WHAT TO DO
WHEN MACHINES
DO EVERYTHING

WHAT TO DO
WHEN MACHINES DO EVERYTHING

HOW TO GET AHEAD IN A WORLD OF AI, ALGORITHMS, BOTS, AND BIG DATA

MALCOLM FRANK, PAUL ROEHRIG, AND BEN PRING

WILEY

Contents

Preface

We know what you might be thinking: When machines do everything, what am *I* going to do? It's a good question.

If machines can do everything, then how are *humans* going to make a living? How are we going to pay the rent or mortgage or put food on the table? How are we going to survive when software eats all the knowledge work?

Even if you have reached a stage in your career in which you feel safe from the rise of the new machines, how will your children thrive when computers can out-think, out-work, and out-manage them? What do they study? Where do they focus? And will they have any chance of living a life as good as yours?

At work, how should your company be structured when so much can now be automated? What will happen to all those middle-class, middle-management knowledge jobs that currently stand as the economic bedrock of our society?

These are all good questions—the right questions—for indeed, something very big is going on.

The rise of artificial intelligence is the great story of our time. Decades in the making, the smart machine is leaving the laboratory and, with increasing speed, is infusing itself into many aspects of our lives: our phones, our cars, the planes we fly in, the way we bank, and the way we choose what music to listen to.

Within the next few years, AI will be all around us, embedded in many higher-order pursuits. It will educate our children, heal our sick, and lower our energy bills. It will catch criminals, increase crop yields, and help us uncover new worlds of augmented and virtual reality.

Machines are getting smarter every day and doing more and more; they will soon change our lives and our work in ways that are easy to imagine but hard to predict. So what does one do?

These are the questions that have been going through our minds for a while, too. Anyone with a casual interest in the future can see these issues swirling through the zeitgeist at the moment: in movies (*Ex Machina* and *Her*), on TV (*Black Mirror, Humans,* and *Battlestar Galactica*), in books (*Superintelligence* and *Rise of the Robots*), and in countless articles in the press. But we have more than a casual interest in the future.

As the leaders of Cognizant's Center for the Future of Work, it is our job to figure out how the future of work works. We engage with many of the world's leading companies, universities, analysts, technologists, and economists to make sense of the great change we are all experiencing as well as to fathom how work will be reimagined, reconfigured, and restructured in the years to come. We do this to understand how new technology will shape the opportunities we have and the threats we face and to foresee how man and machine will relate and coexist.

So we've spent the last three years thinking about what to do when machines do everything, separating the hype from the reality on the front lines of global business.

The book you're holding contains our answers to these questions.

The bottom line? It's going to be all right. In fact, better than all right, because AI is about to usher in a new industrial revolution that, for those who manage it properly, will generate significant economic growth.

Will the new machines displace many current workers? Yes. However, on a larger scale, new machines will also create work that is better, more productive, more satisfying than ever before. The new machines will raise living standards and usher in a period of widely distributed economic growth that will be far stronger than any we've seen in the Western world during the past 50 years.

But there's a catch, which is expressed in the "what to do" part of the title of this book.

You and the company you work for and represent must accept, embrace, and leverage the fact that, minute by minute, machines are doing more and more of the work we perform today. That is the underlying assumption at the heart of this book.

This is where many people get stuck. They start tumbling down existential wormholes: Will machines need us? Who will control the machines? Will machines act in the best interests of humanity? Again, these are great questions that prompt fascinating discussions, all of which we like having as much as the next person, particularly with a glass of red wine on hand. But these discussions don't help you know what to do.

If you want to read about the big philosophical debates about what AI *might* do in the next 25 years, this is not the book for you. But if you want pragmatic advice on what AI *will* do in the next five years, then this is definitely the book for you.

While some have their heads in the sky, others have their noses to the grindstone. While some will ponder, winners will act.

This book aims to answer questions about the future of your business and your work in an era of intelligent machines. It explains how you as an individual and as a leader in your organization can survive and thrive in a world where machines do everything. This book explains what you should do, why, and what will happen if you don't.

We wrote this book because we are in an amazing time. Though we are professional students of the future, the three of us are students of history as well. Understanding the great shifts of the past provides a framework for understanding how change happens in the here and now. The rise of machine intelligence is such a moment of great change. Our children and grandchildren will study these times just as we study James Watt, Andrew Carnegie, and Thomas Edison.

It's time to build our own future, complete with a sense of optimism and confidence. When machines do everything, there will still be a lot for you to do. Let's get on with it.

1

When Machines Do Everything

Artificial intelligence has left the laboratory (and the movie lot) and is in your building. It's in your home. It's in your office. It's pervading all the institutions that drive our global economy. From Alexa to Nest to Siri to Uber to Waze, we are surrounded by smart machines running on incredibly powerful and self-learning software platforms. And this is just the beginning.

To date, we've been enjoying—without even really noticing—various forms of "weak" artificial intelligence (AI). It's how Amazon recommends just the right gift. How Netflix suggests the perfect film for your Sunday evening. Or how Facebook fills your newsfeed. These forms of AI have been welcome little helpers, making our days just a bit easier and more fun. Once we start using them we stop thinking about them. In just a few short years, these machines have become almost invisible to us in our personal lives.

Now AI is transitioning from being our little daily helper to something much more powerful—and disruptive—as the new machines are rapidly outperforming the most talented of us in many endeavors. For example:

- **Games of intellect:** AI platforms can now out-compete us at some of our most challenging games—Jeopardy!, Chess, and Go. Google's AlphaGo beat world champion Go player Lee Sedol by a score of 4–1 in March 2016.[1] This was a convincing win, but not a rout. Yet with the current rate of technological advancement, in just a few years it will be inconceivable for a human to beat the new machines in such games of the mind.
- **Driving:** The driverless car, while still relatively nascent, is already a better driver than the average person. According to a Virginia Tech study, human-driven vehicles are involved in 4.2 crashes per million miles vs. 3.2 crashes per million miles for the automated car.[2] This disparity in safety will undoubtedly grow considerably in the next few years, and driverless cars, which never text behind the wheel or drive drunk, may soon become mainstream.
- **Trading:** In 2015, six of the top eight hedge funds in the United States earned around $8 billion based largely—or exclusively—on AI algorithms.[3] The machine has already won in stock picking.
- **Health care:** In medicine, the new machine is quickly surpassing the capabilities of human radiologists. Researchers at Houston Methodist Hospital utilize AI software, which interprets results of breast X-rays 30 times faster than doctors and with 99% accuracy. By contrast, mammograms reviewed by humans result in unnecessary biopsies nearly 20% of the time.[4]
- **Law:** In the legal profession, AI-enhanced computer systems are conducting discovery and due diligence far better, faster, and cheaper than the most talented team of paralegals in a white-shoe law firm. Multiple studies predict that the vast majority of paralegal work can soon be automated. We may reach a point in the not-too-distant future when relying only on humans for discovery might be grounds for malpractice.

We could go on and on with many more examples, but the point is clear; the new machines have already surpassed human capability in many ways. Moreover, with the geometric growth in the power and sophistication of these platforms, this is only a preview of coming attractions.

Thus, this rapid expansion of AI leads us to ask some big questions:

- Will a robot take my job away?
- Will my company be "Ubered"?
- What will my industry look like in 10 years?
- Will my children be better off than I am?

In the coming pages, we will answer these questions in a structured and practical manner. Based on our cumulative 100 years of experience analyzing and charting shifts in business and technology, we are fully convinced that we're now moving into a new economic era, one that will change the nature of work and the basis of competition in every industry. In this new economy, we will witness an expansion of what is possible and move from machines that do to machines that appear to learn and think.

Like It or Not, This Is Happening

What the World Economic Forum hailed in 2016 as the Fourth Industrial Revolution is now upon us: a time of economic dislocation, when old ways of production give way to new ones, and when those who can harness the power of the new machine will harvest the bounty of economic expansion.[5] In the same manner that the First Industrial Revolution was powered by the invention of the loom, the second by the steam engine, and the third by the assembly line, the fourth will be powered by machines that seem to think—what we refer to in these pages as "systems of intelligence."

This is leading to what we call the "know-it-all" business, in which leaders and managers can and should have a continuous awareness of all that is occurring in their company's operations. Where we used to guess, now we can know. These new machines—always "on," always "learning," and constantly "thinking"—will soon challenge and enhance the intellect and experience of even the savviest professionals in every sector. There's no way to escape the gravitational pull of these new machines and the business models that enable and leverage them.

As such, whether you are managing a large enterprise or just starting your first job, deciding what to do about the new machine—this new cocktail of AI, algorithms, bots, and big data—will be the single biggest determinant of your future success.

Digital That Matters

For the past decade, we've collectively enjoyed "digital that's fun." We've seen the incorporation of Twitter (2006), the introduction of Apple's iPhone (2007), and Facebook's IPO (2012). These companies, along with others, such as Google, Netflix, and Amazon, have been able to generate unprecedented commercial success in terms of customer adoption, daily usage, and value creation by changing how we communicate and socialize. Yet, history will note that we started the digital revolution with the amusing and the frivolous: Facebook posts, Twitter feeds, and Instagram photos. We are using the most powerful innovations since the introduction of alternating current to share cat videos, chat with Aunt Alice, and hashtag political rants. However, that's just the warm-up act, for we haven't yet begun to fully realize the potential of the new machines.

Technology writer Kara Swisher summed it up best when she said, "In Silicon Valley, there's lots of big minds chasing small ideas."[6] Well, we're entering an era of big brains focused on *big* ideas—*digital that matters*—using these technologies to transform how we are educated, fed, transported, insured, medicated, and governed.

While companies such as Facebook, Amazon, Netflix, and Google (sometimes known as the FANG vendors) seem to have established themselves as the presumptive and eternal winners in this space, history will likely remember them as the precursors to a much more momentous and democratic economic shift. The next wave of digital titans probably won't be characterized by start-ups from Silicon Valley; instead, it will be made up of established companies in more "traditional" industries—in places like Baltimore, Birmingham, Berlin, and Brisbane—that figure out how to leverage their longstanding industry knowledge with the power of new machines.

We're starting to see this play out as we collectively work to apply systems of intelligence to help address some of our most vexing societal ills in areas where digital technology is not just entertaining or convenient but also life-altering. Certainly, many of our institutions—the pillars of our society and our everyday lives—are ripe for improvement.

For example, worldwide we lose 1.2 million lives to car accidents annually, with more than 94% of these accidents a result of human error.[7] In the United States alone, these wrecks cost society over $1 trillion. This is nearly one-third the amount the U.S. federal government collects in individual income taxes.[8] Driverless cars promise to save countless lives and heartache.

One-third of all food produced in the world goes to waste. The food wasted in rich countries alone is almost enough to feed all of sub-Saharan Africa.[9] By instrumenting the supply chain and applying AI, we could literally feed the world.

Medical misdiagnoses could also plummet. Right now, 5% to 10% of trips to the ER results in a misdiagnosis.[10] More than 12 million diagnostic mistakes contribute to 400,000 deaths caused by preventable errors each year, and that's just in the United States.[11] Applying data to the diagnostic process could dramatically improve patient outcomes.

The United States spends more per student on secondary education than most other countries in the world but generates mediocre results. In a recent international study, American students achieved scores far below those in many other advanced industrial nations in science, reading, and math.[12] By tailoring lessons to the individual learning style of each student through technology, we could make the education process radically more productive and effective for both students and teachers.

These are the sorts of big things that we can address with the new machine. It's digital with purpose and digital that matters, and the big brains bringing these innovations forward will not necessarily reside in Silicon Valley or an MIT dorm room. They may well be sitting in an office down the hall at your company.

For example, McGraw-Hill Education is applying new technology to help teachers and kids improve learning with a system called ALEKS. The artificially intelligent **A**ssessment and **LE**arning in **K**nowledge **S**paces system uses adaptive questioning to quickly and accurately determine exactly what a student knows and doesn't know in a course. ALEKS then instructs the student on the topics he or she is most ready to learn. As the student works through a course, ALEKS periodically reassesses the student to ensure retention. All of this results in more flexible, one-on-one instruction for students, which boosts student success. And for teachers, ALEKS helps take over some of the more routine—and, let's say it, boring—work to allow them to focus more intently on working with students. Discovery, one of South Africa's leading insurers, uses its Vitality platform to provide economic incentives—discounts on travel, entertainment, healthy food, gym memberships, sports equipment, health products, and the like—to its members based on whether they participate in healthy behaviors. Members earn points by logging workouts with connected fitness devices and purchasing healthy food (also logged by swiping their Vitality card). The insurance sector may not be known as a hotbed of innovation, but Discovery has built a thriving business based on the value derived from the new machine.

Playing the New Game

Another area ripe for reinvention is managing our money. Jon Stein doesn't look like a Wall Street Master of the Universe—just the opposite, in fact. In his mid-30s, dressed in blue jeans and a mildly tattered shirt, he works not in a financial citadel but in a relaxed loft-like space. His language is not full of bravado and bombast but is casual, considered, and humble.

Yet Stein is turning his corner of the banking world, personal wealth management, on its head. His company, Betterment, has rapidly become one

Figure 1.1   Jon Stein, CEO and founder of Betterment

of the world's leading "robo-advisors," leveraging AI platforms to rewrite the rules of the financial advisory business. Betterment provides highly personalized, curated wealth management services 24x7. His system of intelligence is doing the work of hundreds of people and is doing it better, at a fraction of the cost.

Millions of investors—millennials, Gen-Xers, and baby boomers alike—are flocking to the platform. From the beginning of 2015 to mid-2016, Betterment's assets under management grew from $1.1 billion to $5.0 billion[13,14] and for good reason. Betterment has created a bigger pie for wealth management services because it can attract new customers that traditional banks wouldn't touch. Traditional "bulge-bracket" investment banks (e.g., Goldman Sachs, Morgan Stanley, Credit Suisse, etc.) often do not offer personalized wealth management services to anyone with less than $1 million in assets; the margin isn't there, given their one-to-one advisory business model. So where does that leave the other 99.9% of the population that is interested in having their money professionally managed?

Betterment started by focusing on HENRY (*high earners, not rich yet*). These are young professionals in their 20s and early 30s: lawyers, doctors, and managers starting their careers armed with great educations . . . and the associated student debt.

Traditional wealth managers won't touch HENRY, but Betterment welcomes anyone with money to invest. And as each new customer comes on the platform, the system gets smarter, providing better value to each individual participant: on the spot, empirically based, unspun counsel on investment strategy, portfolio allocation, and tax management.

Robo-advisers, collectively, have more than $50 billion in assets under management today (and are estimated to have over $250 billion under management by 2020) and are taking aim at the $20 trillion worldwide that is currently being managed by 46,000 human financial advisors at traditional banks.[15]

Now, we don't know whether Betterment will ultimately emerge as the long-term winner in this new form of financial advisory services, but the company does demonstrate how new machines are disrupting traditional ways of work. Such widespread adoption is creating shock waves in both the financial services and technology industries.

Stein, and others who have figured out the new game, are nothing short of the Henry Fords of our time. They understand today's new raw materials (big data). They have built and now operate the new machines. And, most important, they have surrounded these new machines with business models that generate remarkable growth and profitability engines while expanding the overall market.

The story of robo-advisors in wealth management is about to be replayed a thousand-fold across all sectors of our economy. So the question becomes: Will you play, or stand on the sidelines?

But Will *I* Be Automated Away?

We have already proven that we love to consume AI-based products (with our rabid usage of the FANG vendors' offers on our smartphones). And, through digital that matters, the new machine is poised to transform the primary institutions of our society for the better.

Yet once we get over our initial awe of the new machine, we start to wonder how it will impact jobs. What will happen to all those bankers, drivers, radiologists, lawyers, and journalists? What will happen to . . . me? Will a robot take my job?

Many of us don't know whether this Fourth Industrial Revolution is very good or very bad. It all starts to feel like a capitalist's dream . . . but a worker's nightmare. And the uncertainty is creating a palpable sense of anxiety, for at a personal level, many of us don't know what to do about it.

Some see only the dark side of this shift, and indeed, many of today's headlines forecast a grim future in a "jobless economy" as robots take over our livelihoods. But the coming digital boom and build-out we describe in the next chapter will be highly promising for those who are prepared. In fact, it will usher in once-in-a-century growth prospects as we reengineer our infrastructure, our industries, and our institutions. Similar to the prior three industrial revolutions, this one will steamroll those who wait and watch, and will unleash enormous prospects and prosperity for those who learn to harness the new machine.

All of this depends on what *you do now* to prepare for an era when machines can potentially do nearly everything related to knowledge work.

Will many jobs be "automated away" in the coming years? Yes. However, for the vast majority of professions, the new machine will actually enhance and protect employment. We don't think, for example, that a single teacher or nurse will lose their job due to artificial intelligence. Instead, these professions will become more productive, more effective . . . and more enjoyable. Workers in such professions will come to view the new machine as their trusted colleague. Just as one wouldn't think of driving across London today without an AI-based GPS, or researching a subject without referring to Google and Wikipedia, most workers in the coming years would not consider approaching their daily tasks without a "bot" at their side.

Additionally, entirely new professions will be created, driving employment in fields we can't currently envision (imagine trying to describe a "database administrator" to somebody in 1955). We have much to look forward to *if* we understand exactly what the new machine can and cannot do and how it will impact the future of work. Some very clear patterns for success have emerged, and we'll spend the rest of the book framing what's going on and providing tactical guidance on how to win in the new digital economy.

Getting AHEAD in the Age of the New Machine

We've written this book to provide you with a roadmap, a guide to success for this time of transition. First, we will outline what the machine actually is: how it's built, what it can do, and what it *can't* do. We will then look at where it can best be used today and tomorrow. What industry problems can it solve? What new customer value propositions can it create? Third, and most importantly, we will give you a structured approach for moving forward with our AHEAD model, which is based on our work with Global 2000 companies at the vanguard of the digital transition.

Briefly, AHEAD outlines the five distinct approaches for winning with systems of intelligence. The acronym stands for:

- **Automate:** Outsource rote, computational work to the new machine. This is how Netflix automated away the Blockbuster retail store and how Uber is automating away taxi dispatching.
- **Halo:** Instrument products and people and leverage the data exhaust they generate through their connected and online behaviors (what we call Code Halos) to create new customer experiences and business models.[16] General Electric and Nike are changing the rules of the game in their industries by instrumenting their products, surrounding

them with halos of data, and creating new value propositions and customer intimacy.

- **Enhance:** View the computer as a colleague that can increase your job productivity and satisfaction. The GPS in your car currently enhances your driving, keeping you on the fastest route, alerting you of road hazards, and ensuring that you never get lost. In the coming years, entire vocations, from sales to nursing to teaching, will be revolutionized with the power of computer-based enhancement.
- **Abundance:** Use the new machine to open up vast new markets by dropping the price point of existing offers, much as Henry Ford did with automobiles. In the way that Betterment is using AI to bring financial security to the masses, which market offers can be greatly democratized and expanded in your industry?
- **Discovery:** Leverage AI to conceive entirely new products, new services, and entirely new industries. As Edison's light bulb led to new discoveries in radio, television, and transistors, today's new machine will lead to a new generation of discovery and invention.

These are five specific approaches—*plays*, if you will—for winning with AI, each with its own set of approaches and tactics. In the coming pages, we will utilize this model to demystify the application of the new machine in your business.

The first play—*to automate*—is the one most prevalent in today's zeitgeist. Automation has been the initial step in each industrial revolution, as one loom replaced 40 textile workers or one steam engine had the power of 50 horses. Today, automation will be a similar necessary "evil," because it's how you will deliver at the "Google price" in core portions of your company. However, what most market observers miss is that the next wave of automation will pave the way for invention and economic expansion through the four subsequent plays.

This one-two of efficiency plus invention will manifest itself across all industries. Banking will become more efficient and personalized. Health care will become more transparent and effective, generating much better outcomes. Manufactured goods will become more interactive, intuitive, and reliable. Our food system will be less wasteful and produce higher quality goods. Education will be enhanced and individualized, and government services will be upgraded and more cost-effective. And, as outlined previously, much of this shift will not be driven by companies that were started last year or even 10 years ago but by companies started by our grandparents. This is because those companies have access to the richest lodes of data, the "fuel" for the new machine.

Much has already been said and written about the potential impact of the new machine on society. We wrote this book not for policy wonks and academics but rather for people in organizations large and small that are trying to make the best decisions possible for their businesses and their own jobs. We aren't naïve to the fact that business happens in a wider context, but we can't all sit around waiting for politicians to improve education or to pass huge spending bills to enhance infrastructure or enact a universal basic income. We need to act *today* in the world as it is. You can rest assured that if you don't act now, others will.

The title of this book is *What to Do When Machines Do Everything*. This may sound a bit hyperbolic, and clearly machines will never do *everything* and nobody really wants them to. But in the next few years the new machines will continue to amaze, will be embedded most everywhere and in most everything, and will increasingly do more and more of the work people do today.

Technology is no longer the domain of the few but the province of the many. As such, those who win in the next phase of the digital economy are not those who can create the new machines, but those who figure out what to do with them. This book is your field guide.

2 | From Stall to Boom

We've Been Here Before

Many of us feel stalled. Growth, both for our companies and for us individually, seems increasingly difficult to attain. There is plenty of evidence of the structural weakening of our economy: stagnant wages, rising debt levels, and anemic productivity growth. It seems the major trends are all working against us: increased global competition, a winner-take-all economy driving massive income inequality, the steady erosion of privacy and security, start-ups worth billions emerging while legacy firms crumble, and technology taking our jobs. It's clear that the old rules of work and business no longer apply.

We (the authors) work with a lot of people excited about the opportunities that lie ahead in the digital economy, but their optimism is often tempered by the news of the day. The headlines all too frequently seem to foretell a pending jobless nightmare of breadlines and robot overlords. And some feel as if there's a party being thrown—in Silicon Valley, New York, and London—that they're not invited to.

Yet within the malaise there is good news. We have weathered similar storms before, and the shape and pattern of our current situation is actually a harbinger for a period of technology-fueled growth. This seems counter-intuitive; after all, how can economic stagnation signal future growth and opportunity?

It's because our current stall fits within a well-established pattern that shows up during every major shift in business and technology, when the economy moves from one industrial revolution to the next. In short, we are currently in an economic "stall zone" as the Third Industrial Revolution is (literally) running out of gas, while the Fourth Industrial Revolution—based on the new machine—has yet to grab hold at scale.

This situation creates a dissonance in which we marvel at the computers that surround us, and all they can do, while we search in vain for greater growth prospects for our companies and career security for ourselves.

The good news, which we will explore in this chapter, is that we are coming to the end of the stall zone and entering a time when the economy can break out for those who harness the power of the new machine. We refer to this as the coming "digital build-out," in which the fruits of digital technology move from Silicon Valley to the entire economy. This value migration will be of a scale similar to the industrial build-out of the last century and will move much faster. To fully understand this transition, it helps to take a look back at the impact of new machines on work in previous periods of tumultuous disruption.

When Machines Do Everything, What Happens to Us?

People have been worried about "new machines" and their effect on the human condition for centuries. Only the machine has changed; the concerns remain the same.

Back in the early 1800s, during the First Industrial Revolution, the Luddites in northwestern England responded to the introduction of power looms by smashing them. They recognized that their textile jobs were at risk. It turned out that they were right; the machines *did* take over their jobs. Then the same thing happened in agriculture. At the beginning of the 19th century—when the Luddites were smashing looms—80% of the U.S. labor force was working the land. Today, less than 2% of U.S. workers are in agriculture.

Figure 2.1   Luddites in the early 1800s

When the steam engine enabled mechanization during the Second Industrial Revolution, experts openly worried that "the substitution of machinery for human labor" might "render the population redundant."[1] As assembly lines made mass production possible, the economist John Maynard Keynes famously warned about widespread unemployment, "due to our discovery of means of economizing the use of labor outrunning the pace at which we can find new uses for labor."[2]

Today, many of us feel that same sense of trepidation as we read increasingly foreboding accounts of how new machines based on artificial intelligence will displace us. A widely cited Oxford University study estimates that nearly 50% of total U.S. jobs are at risk from the new machines during the next decade or so.[3]

But Haven't Our Computers Made Us More Productive?

In spite of this doom and gloom, some of us, being ever-optimistic, will argue, "Maybe so. But all of these computers are having a broad positive effect as they are making all of us more productive." However, the data doesn't support this argument either.

In spite of the billions spent on enterprise technology (think of all those Cisco routers, SAP applications, Oracle databases, and Microsoft-based PCs, combined with the recent explosion in consumer technologies such as smartphones and apps) worker productivity and associated G7 industrialized nation GDPs haven't budged much. For example, from 1991 through 2012 the average annual increase in real wages was a paltry 1.5% in the UK and 1% in the United States (which was approximately half the level of wage growth from 1970 through 1990), and these were the *leaders* in wage growth in the industrialized world.[4] Similarly, GDP growth rates in the United States and Western Europe during those two decades were *below* the GDP growth rates of the previous two decades.[5]

How can this be? How is it that we are merely treading economic water in spite of massive technology investments? Isn't this a technology golden age?

Ask yourself: Have your PC, smartphone, e-mail, and instant messaging platforms shortened your work day? Ours neither.

Carlota's Way

The good news amid the gloom is that our current stall zone fits a historical pattern that foretells future growth. Indeed, the signals of fear that the new machine will take our jobs usually appear at the cusp of technology-led economic booms. In fact, if the Fourth Industrial Revolution doesn't generate widespread economic expansion along with associated job growth, we will have broken with history. Why do we have confidence in such a prediction? A Venezuelan-born economist will help guide us.

Carlota Perez is an award-winning economics professor at the London School of Economics. Her most important work focuses on what happens *between* the end of one era and the beginning of the next. She describes it like this:

> *History can teach us a lot. Innovation has indeed always been the driver of growth and the main source of increasing productivity and wealth. But every technological revolution has brought two types of prosperity.*

The first type is turbulent and exciting like the bubbles of the 1990s and 2000s and like the Roaring Twenties, the railway mania, and the canal mania before. They all ended in a bubble collapse.

Yet, after the recession, there came the second type: the Victorian boom, the Belle Époque, the Post War Golden Age and . . . the one that we could have ahead now.

Bubble prosperities polarize incomes; Golden Ages tend to reverse the process.[6]

Perez describes a coming Golden Age, the digital build-out that's just in front of us. But we're getting ahead of ourselves. How and why can this emerge from our current economic stall? The patterns of history provide us with the guide.

Riding the Waves

When we look back at the invention of the cotton gin, the internal combustion engine, and alternating current, we might sometimes think that one day there was an invention and the next day everything changed. But that's not how the world works. In virtually every case, there was a long and bumpy road connecting one era of business and technology to the next; the evolution of each industrial revolution follows the path of an *S-curve* (as shown in Figure 2.2).

Why an S-curve? Historically, upon the introduction of new technologies, associated GDP does not rise for decades (the bottom of the S-curve).

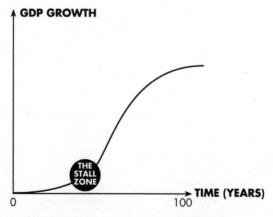

Figure 2.2   The S-Curve and the Stall Zone

Select individuals and companies might get rich, but society overall does not. Yet once the technology fully grabs hold, usually 25 to 35 years into the cycle, GDP experiences near-vertical liftoff (the middle of the S-curve). All current members of the G7 nations have experienced this previously—for example, Great Britain rode the steam engine to massive GDP growth in the 19th century, and the United States did the same with the assembly line in the 20th century.

Over time, as the technology is fully adopted and finds its way into most every industry and part of the globe, GDP growth wanes (the top of the S-curve). This is where we are today with the industrial economy of the Third Industrial Revolution. The model of production is well understood, widely distributed, and commoditized. (Consider, for example, the nearly 23 million motorcycles produced in China in 2013.)[7] This top-of-the-curve, flattening-out is what's behind our current economic malaise.

This S-curve pattern of innovation, stall, rapid expansion, then maturity has occurred with the previous three industrial revolutions, and to date it's playing out in the early stages of our computer-driven Fourth Industrial Revolution (as shown in Figure 2.3.)

Currently we find ourselves at the end of the stall zone and are entering rapid expansion. But this situation of being between stages is also why we

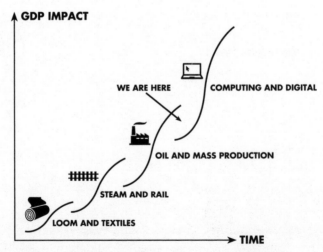

Figure 2.3   S-Curves and Industrial Revolutions

have such confusion in today's markets between the optimistic techno-philes and the pessimistic economists. Both groups are right *if* their aperture is focused on the past 20 years (which, for most observers, is often simply based on their own personal experiences). However, in expanding the view over a broader arc of economic history it becomes very clear as to where we are, where we have been, and (most importantly) where we are headed.

To reinforce this point, let's take a closer look at recent history and how these periods fit within Professor Perez's model.

The Burst of Innovation (1980–2000)

The advent of the PC, Steve Jobs's original Mac, Bill Gates becoming the world's richest person, the Internet explosion, the wiring of our corpora-tions. It was all so very heady. It was "the time of the great happiness" as remembered in the technology industry, at least until it all ended in tears with the dot-com bubble and bust.

Similar bursts of innovation have occurred at the beginning of each industrial revolution, paving the way for the great fortunes of titans such as Cornelius Vanderbilt, Andrew Carnegie, and John D. Rockefeller. But this wealth was highly concentrated, because the new technologies and their associated business models were understood and implemented by only a few. The public at large would marvel at the new machine of its age; it would garner lots of press and capture the collective imagination, yet its reach was still limited and highly concentrated in a few industries and geographies. Invariably, when too much capital would start chasing too few implemen-ters, financial bubbles would result.

The Stall (2000–2015)

The Internet bubble burst around the turn of the millennium. Then, roughly seven years later, the financial crisis hit. And we've been stalled for a decade and a half. While it all felt new and unpleasantly surprising to us, our recent busts and malaise have also fit closely with the historical pattern.

This stall zone, while painful to experience, is an important period of change. Think of it as the gestation period of a new technology, the larva in the cocoon before it becomes a butterfly, during which the broader economy takes time figuring out how to best leverage the new machine and business models catch up with technology innovation.

This is why the FANG vendors, along with unicorns like Dropbox, Airbnb, and Betterment, are so important; they have provided examples of combining the new machine with new business models. Probably more important is to look beyond the FANG vendors to the industrial leaders that have recognized the shift, such as Siemens, Nike, and Progressive Insurance Corporation. These enterprises are making moves that will take time to come to full fruition but will ultimately set them up for success in the digital build-out phase that will follow the stall. In the coming pages, we will decode many of the important lessons to be learned from both FANGs and well-established corporations who are successful early adopters of new machines and business models.

The Build-Out (2015–2040)

This is the phase when innovations move from the radical fringe to the mainstream. It is the time for the "democratization" of the innovation, as new ideas, which are initially implemented in very concentrated areas, become much more widely disseminated.

This will occur over the next few decades, when industries and institutions that serve as the pillars of our society—banking, insurance, health care, education, transportation, law enforcement, government— leverage the power of the new machine and begin to base their operating models on digital technology.

OK, enough of the economic theory. We took this brief trip through history and economics (summarized in Figure 2.4) in order to set the stage for what's happening to all of us currently and to point out that all of the available evidence reveals us to be on a path not to the end of times but to the Fourth Industrial Revolution build-out. Every previous industrial revolution has followed this same basic cycle of innovation bubble, stall, and boom. The digital revolution is no exception, and there are three big reasons for why we are about to transition to widespread, digitally driven growth.

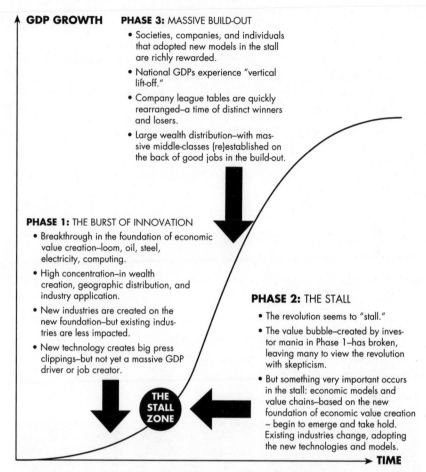

Figure 2.4 The Three Phases of the S-Curve

Three Big Reasons Why a Boom Is About to Occur

As we see it, the transition to the build-out phase will be driven by three parallel large-scale trends:

- **"Ubiquitech"—technology embedded into everything**. As the Internet of Things (IoT) comes to life, almost everything will become tech-infused, connected, and intelligent. When tech is everywhere, transformation can come from anywhere.
- **By 2030 standards, we stink**. In 2030, we will look back at many aspects of today's society and wonder, "How did we tolerate that?" We

have big problems to solve with the new machine, and in the process massive new forms of demand will be generated.

- **Becoming digital—mastering the Three M's (raw Materials, new Machines, and business Models)**. Enterprises are "becoming digital," organizing their people and processes around the capabilities of the new machine. Increasingly, the winning new business models are emerging out of the stall zone, leading to the rearranging of league tables in industry after industry.

Now let's explore all three of these.

"Ubiquitech"—Technology Embedded into Everything

In the next decade, most everything around us will become tech-enabled and connected. The "Internet of Things (IoT)" is the catchall phrase that describes the embedding of computing capability into devices and objects that have previously not had such capacity, and then the connecting of them to the Internet. Think of your shoes, thermostat, or hair dryer; your town's streetlamps and parking meters; and the multiple key components of a jet liner, an assembly line, or a power grid.

Figure 2.5   Our Connected World

In some cases, this digital "enchantment" is relatively limited.[8] For example, a light bulb can now contain a sensor that tells the bulb when it is dark, and thus it turns itself on. In other cases the "thing" is much more sophisticated. An entire house can be wired so that, in effect, it becomes a networked computer—a "smart home." Not only the lights but also doors, windows, temperature, security features, entertainment systems, and kitchen appliances can all be programmed to do things automatically. Further, they all can be controlled when the home owner is five feet—or 5,000 miles—away from home.

The spread of this capability—making every *thing* Internet Protocol addressable—is happening at breakneck speed; the scale of the explosion of the "thing" universe is staggering, and even hard to fully comprehend. For example:

- Cisco Systems estimates that the number of connected devices world-wide will rise to 50 billion by 2020.[9] Intel goes even further, suggesting that over 200 billion devices will be connected by then.[10]
- McKinsey forecasts that global spending on IoT devices and services could reach $11 trillion by 2025.[11]
- With "wearables" constituting an important sub-element of this market, IDC expects global wearable-device shipments to surge from 76.1 million in 2015 to 173.4 million units by 2019.[12]
- The smart-home scenario, mentioned above, will be a significant growth area; according to Harbor Research and Postscapes, it generated $79.4 billion in revenue in 2014 when it was just in its infancy.[13] That number is expected to increase to $398 billion as mainstream awareness of smart appliances rises.[14]
- The auto industry is becoming "smarter" by the day. Even before cars become fully autonomous (i.e., "driverless") they will become more like increasingly connected rolling data centers. By 2020, 90% of cars will be online, compared with just 2% in 2012.[15]
- General Electric estimates that the "Industrial Internet" market will add between $10 trillion and $15 trillion to global GDP within the next 20 years.[16]

Of course, these are all just estimates and should be treated with some degree of cool skepticism. But whatever the actual numbers turn out to be, there is little doubt that the trend lines strikingly point in only one direction. The next generation of smart devices will be hugely significant for nearly every kind of business.

In reality though, we've only scratched the surface of this "smart" wave. We can already see texts and our heart rate on an Apple Watch; sure that's cool, but why can't it do a lot more? Why can't Amazon Alexa manage our whole home? Why can't Nest smart thermostats monitor the house for leaks and other insurance risks? In due course, all of these things will happen, and millions of other similar "smart scenarios" will stop being science fiction and will become, simply, our reality.

But improvements in entertainment and domestic life won't impact the wider economy enough to transition us from stall to boom. What is starting to happen and does have the potential to raise all our boats is the application of IoT ideas to mission-critical parts of the economy, such as health care, transportation, and defense. Such a development has begun to radically change *work that matters*.

We'll look at many more examples of smart devices in Chapter 8; for now, just recognize that soon your default position should be to instrument all of your operations, products, and customer experiences.

By 2030 Standards, We Stink

Just as we tease our parents and grandparents about the outhouse in the back yard, black-and-white television sets, and the cars without seatbelts that were common in their day, our descendants will rib us about how rudimentary and odd our tools still are today. They will look back on us and wonder, "How on earth could they live like that?"

If you have very young children, imagine sitting at dinner with them as teenagers 15 years from now, describing the world they were born into. After their giggles over Justin Bieber, the Kardashians ("What was *that* all about?"), hipster beards, and hashtags, the conversation may move on to more pedestrian issues. For example, you may describe to them what you had to go through to get your car fixed.

You know the scenario, when you go to the service department of your car dealership: you sit there with a dozen strangers, sipping the stale coffee, watching CNN on a TV that's playing about 10 decibels above comfort level. Your mind starts to wander: "How long will this take? Will I make it back to the office in time? And do I really trust what the mechanic is about to tell me about the extent and cost of the repair?" Ten years from now, your car will self-diagnose exactly what is wrong with it, will give you an estimated cost of the repair, and then will schedule itself for an appointment at the dealership based on your calendar. Then, as your car drives itself out of your office's parking lot to get itself repaired, you will start to think of how much we tolerated, and the opportunity costs that abounded, in our pre-digital era.

In 2030, those 15-year-olds will wonder how we didn't know days in advance that we would be coming down with a cold. That every student at school didn't have a highly pixilated understanding of their personal learning style and a supporting individualized curriculum to maximize their development. That when patients arrived at the emergency room they first had to spend time presenting their insurance card and then sitting in the waiting room instead of having their personal health history, as well as pictures and videos of their injury, sent ahead so a team of well-prepared doctors was awaiting them at the door.

Our current industrial-age inefficiencies may feel terrible now, but anyone with an entrepreneurial bone in their body sees problems and friction as business opportunities to *fix* these gaps. New machine-based digital solutions such as these—multiplied across all industries—will address myriad societal problems, in the process generating enormous economic value. Rather than presaging the end of the middle class, technology will help drive massive financial expansion.

The key point is this: in thinking about digital solutions and artificial intelligence, we often focus on the impact of the technology *on the world that we know.* Many critics thus go straight to the "How many jobs will the machine destroy?" question, yet the question is really about "What can this technology improve?" The answer is "a tremendous amount," for in viewing things from a 2030 perspective, it's clear how much is about to change.

To better understand the scope and scale of this opportunity, Cognizant's Center for the Future of Work, together with economists from Roubini ThoughtLab (a leading independent macroeconomic research firm founded by renowned economist Nouriel Roubini) studied 2,000 companies across the globe to understand the economic impact of the new machine. Our study, conducted in early 2016, focused on several industries that are central to our economy but have yet to become truly digital (i.e., retail, banking, insurance [health and property & casualty] manufacturing, and life sciences), which collectively generate over $60 trillion in revenue today (roughly 40% of world GDP).[17]

Respondents reported that approximately 6% of that revenue was currently driven by digital but that the figure will nearly double during the next three years to 11.4%. To put this in perspective, this means the "Republic of Digital," if it existed as a separate country, will soon be a $6.6 trillion economy, making it the third largest economy in the world behind the United States and China and roughly equal to the economic horsepower of the 2015 economies of Germany, the UK, and Austria, combined. As work that matters becomes more fully digitized, leveraging the new AI machines, huge economic expansion is set to occur.

Becoming Digital: Mastering the Three M's

In looking at the digital economy, the consensus view seems to be that recent start-ups shall inherit the earth. After all, who can stop the momentum of relatively young yet already rich and massive companies like Amazon, Google, Facebook, and Uber? Where does this leave the 100-year-old companies, or even the 40-year-old companies? What about them? Actually, in a very good place . . . if they move quickly.

In our view, long established companies are extraordinarily well-positioned for the digital build-out. This is because they already have advantages for taking the steps required on the next leg of the journey in delivering digital that matters. They understand their markets, products, and associated regulations better than anybody. And, per the IoT section, they have all the assets to instrument in order to gain proprietary insights into their operations and markets. Still, to get there they must align the Three M's.

The Three M's refer to (raw) materials, (new) machines, and (business) models. Further along we devote individual chapters examining how each of these elements is necessary for winning in the coming digital boom. For now, the key point is that these three elements have to be *integrated* and *aligned* to create value. Why? Let's look at how the combination of these three elements has driven every major business and technology shift that's come before.

How the Three M's have historically related to each other is illustrated in Figure 2.6.

RAW MATERIALS	MACHINES	BUSINESS MODELS

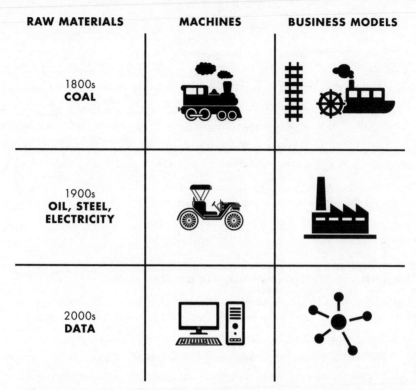

1800s **COAL**		
1900s **OIL, STEEL, ELECTRICITY**		
2000s **DATA**		

Figure 2.6   The Three M's in Major Business and Technology Revolutions

In our current context, the Three M's are:

- **Raw materials:** the data generated from IoT devices and instrumentation of all people, places, and things.
- **New machines:** systems of intelligence that combine hardware, AI software, data, and human input to create value aligned to a specific business process or customer experience.
- **Business models:** commercial models that monetize services and solutions based on systems of intelligence.

Perhaps the best example of aligning the Three M's comes from a company that is well over 100 years old.

Today, many mythologize Henry Ford as having invented the car. He didn't. When Ford launched the Ford Motor Company it was actually his *third* car company (the first had failed and the second became Cadillac), and he had dozens of competitors in Detroit alone, including Oldsmobile, Packard, and Buick.

What Henry Ford did invent, his great gift, was the alignment of the Three M's of his time, with a primary focus on the third; he created a business model based on the assembly line, which completely changed the price and quality points of the automobile. Aligning the Three M's allowed Ford to mass-produce cars (turning them from a toy for the rich into a necessity for the masses), win his competitive battles, reshape transportation, and reshape society.

In subsequent chapters, we'll discuss how the Three M's will impact your organization and your work in more detail.

New Business Models Take Shape in the Stall Zone

The stall zone is vitally important because materials and machines are understood long before the associated business models can adapt.

The starting point for a truly digital business model, or for the specific business process or customer experience in question, should not be "How do we make it better/faster/cheaper by adding new technology to it?" Instead, the question should be "If digital technologies were available when we designed this process, would we have structured it differently?" The former lens gives you Blockbuster, which put Internet e-commerce on top of a retail chain network. The latter lens yields Netflix, which designed core processes as digital from the ground up.

General Electric currently stands out as an industrial leader that is undergoing the hard work of reconfiguring itself around the Three M's for the digital economy. Incorporated in 1892, GE is the oldest company listed on the New York Stock Exchange, so you couldn't find a better poster child of an old-school industrial company. It retains its leadership in manufacturing power turbines, jet engines, lighting, and locomotives, but it is currently becoming so much more.

GE CEO Jeff Immelt recognized the need to combine data, systems of intelligence, and new business models to win in the digital industrial economy. He noted, "If you went to bed last night as an industrial company, you're going to wake up this morning as a software and analytics company."[18]

Leaders at GE are taking tactical steps to make the shift to the Fourth Industrial Revolution happen by creating what they refer to as "the world's premier digital industrial company." In recent years, they have jumped fully into ubiquitech, putting sensors into nearly every "thing" they make to generate the new raw material. GE has invested in building an IoT management platform (Predix), which is the company's system of intelligence. And GE hasn't overlooked new business models. It is now selling insights based on the raw material, opening up entirely new lines of business. In fact, GE now has a software business earning more than $6 billion in revenue, making it one of the world's largest software companies.[19]

Another example of a 100-year-old industry realigning itself around the Three M's model, and leveraging the new machine, is education, which certainly is a pillar of society where progress is badly needed, long overdue, and finally coming into focus. We met with Joel Rose, co-founder of New Classrooms Innovation Partners, whose work is a leading indicator of a Three M–aligned future. Rose is trying with new tools, machines, and attitudes to reinvent a hidebound industry and mindset seemingly unchanged since long before many of us were in school.

Developing People of Intelligence with Systems of Intelligence

The notion of "reinventing education" has a long and bumpy history that predates the advent of the computer but has certainly accelerated since PCs found their way into schools during the late 1970s. Space prohibits us from revisiting too much of that history here, but suffice to say most of it ends badly!

Launched in 2011 by teachers, education administrators, and technologists, New Classrooms is essentially leveraging the power of data to tailor teaching individually and thus break the long-established educational norm: a teacher standing in front of a class of 30 students, all of them learning the same material at the same time. That traditional teaching model is literally an *industrial* model. Large-scale public education dates from a time when workers were pouring into factories and mills, and it mirrors the production-line mentality that was key to efficiency and productivity within those then-new technology spaces.

In a New Classrooms school, students equipped with laptops or tablets are placed in groups of typically between 5 and 20, and work through assignments and projects where they undertake different "modalities" of learning at "stations" within the classroom; some modalities have the kids collaborate in teams, some directly with a teacher, some "virtually" with online software programs. At the stations, teachers interact with the group, answering questions, setting challenges, or posing new questions. After each interaction, the group moves on to another assignment and visits new stations. Whereas a traditional school will have one group of 30 kids interact in one room with one teacher, a New Classrooms school will have between two and six teachers as well as additional team educators in a large space or several classrooms with between 60 and 80 kids circulating amongst the stations (see Figure 2.7).

All the lessons are online (though it should be noted that not all the teaching happens exclusively through a computer). Most of the

Figure 2.7   A Typical New Classrooms Learning Environment

grading is done automatically and in a fraction of the time a human teacher would require, and by 6 A.M. the following day, each student, along with the associated teachers, receives a fully individualized learning plan for the day ahead. This outline is based on the software's analysis of the student's progress: what needs a do-over, what needs reinforcement, and what new input can be added to stretch and engage the student.

New Classrooms co-founder Joel Rose says the main issue with the *industrial* teaching model is that in a class of 30 students, the three brightest kids will be bored to death, the 10 least academically gifted will be hopelessly lost (and perhaps prone to causing mischief), and the kids in the middle will muddle through, some doing well through inclination (or with the help of parental carrots and sticks) and some drifting in and out of the process. In a New Classrooms school, steered by data and machine learning and platforms, the "no back rows" philosophy of a private academy is made available to students in a public school environment; no students fall through the proverbial cracks. The New Classrooms model is thus bringing the concept of the "democratization of luxury" to life in an arena that is vital to us all, individually and societally.

The team at New Classrooms is all too conscious of the inertia surrounding them, but they report the growing numbers of principals, teachers, boards, and parents who are open to the radical reengineering of both the physical classroom and the "workflow" of learning.

From Stall to Boom, a Time of Optimism

The three of us have been working at the cutting edge of business and technology for years. If you ask people who know us, we could hardly be accused of being naïve or irrationally exuberant about any specific technology. Even so, we have a sense of optimism based on what we see happening in the market, among our customers, and from our research. Essentially, this is what this book is about: getting *you* to the prosperity found in the coming digital build-out. The primary thing you need to take away from this chapter is the necessity of (a) understanding the new machine and (b) situating it in the right business model. This is the heart of our thesis, and in the coming chapters we detail (and demystify) each of the Three M's in today's success formula and explain how they must be activated to move ahead.

But before we get to that we need to address "the elephant" in our book, the great concerns we've mentioned that many have about the impact of AI and automation on jobs.

3 | There Will Be Blood

So far, our narrative has been generally positive. We believe the new machines will help us move our companies and our economies from stall to boom. But this transition won't be without significant disruption in jobs. Metaphorically, there will be blood.

The rise of the new machine poses a difficult question: Is it a capitalist's dream or a worker's nightmare? Or both? At the dawn of the Fourth Industrial Revolution, many people are asking, "How many solid, middle-class office worker jobs will soon be eliminated?"

This is no abstract consideration, for there's probably a voice inside you wondering "Will new disruptive technologies take *my* job away? And, even if my job is safe, what about the ethical implications of automation sending many of my colleagues to the unemployment line?"

Predictions of Massive Job Losses via AI

No doubt such concerns have been amplified by recent headlines on the potential impact of AI on employment. After all, some predict that robotic automation will eliminate enormous portions of the workforce. Oxford University researchers have predicted as many as 47% of U.S. jobs could be automated away by 2025.[1]

There are about 160 million jobs in the entire U.S. workforce, so the Oxford prediction would mean roughly 75 million jobs would simply be gone.[2] Extrapolated across the G7 industrialized nations, where there are roughly 368 million jobs, this would mean at least 173 million jobs would be eviscerated by the new machine within eight years. Such levels of unemployment occurring at such a pace would lead us to an *Elysium*-class dystopian future.[3]

Of course, *some* jobs will be automated away, but 173 million G7 jobs by 2025? We don't think so. 173 million is such a large number it does not pass the smell test, for that's larger than the entire population of Russia, or the combined workforces of Germany, the UK, France, Italy, Australia, and Canada.

Take a deep breath. The rise of the new machine is not going to lead to full-scale revolution in the streets. A lot of jobs, indeed, millions of jobs over time, will be automated but not at a scale or pace that will create the social dislocation that some are predicting (and many more are fearing).

There are literally dozens of studies on this topic, and in reviewing nearly every one of them over the past three years we have found that the Oxford report takes the most extreme position. Not surprisingly, it has grabbed most of the headlines as it has tapped the nerve of insecurity in our slow-growth, stalled economy.

The consensus among the majority of the studies, though, is far less dramatic, positing a range from around 5% to 15% of jobs being automated away over the coming 10 to 15 years. Based on our analysis, we believe that the middle of this range, about 12%, is the most likely scenario.

This level of job dislocation from AI of course is still significant. 12% is the equivalent of around 19 million jobs in the United States. If one of those jobs is yours, life will undoubtedly be very tough. However, what's often overlooked in examining the big picture of employment levels is the growth of new jobs. We believe that there will be almost 21 million new jobs, about 13% of the current U.S. labor force, directly created as a result of the growth of the new machine. In case these numbers—19 million jobs disappearing and 21 million jobs being created—sound implausible, keep in mind, as a point of reference, that since 2010, during the years of the post–Great Recession recovery, 15 million private sector jobs have been created in the United States.

Our assumption is that in the industrialized world, for nations that embrace the Fourth Industrial Revolution, unemployment rates by 2025 will be roughly what they are today.[4] This relatively small expected change—plus or minus—in the net unemployment rate will, however, mask huge changes in what work we do and how we do it. Within the overall labor force, there will be massive job transition (often creating skills mismatches), and figuring out "what to do" within this churn is what this book is all about.

The new machine will change the G7 labor force in three distinct ways:

1. **Job automation:** Roughly 12% of existing jobs are at risk of being taken over by systems of intelligence.
2. **Job enhancement:** Roughly 75% of existing jobs will be altered or enhanced by the bot. The employment will remain, and these jobs will be delivered with greater output and/or quality.
3. **Job creation:** 13% net new jobs will be created as the new machine creates new revenue opportunities and/or new job categories.

In our view, any responsible analysis of the impact of the bot on jobs needs to consider job automation, enhancement, and creation together; new machines always give as much as they take away.

We believe that the more fearful predictions are based on research that is incomplete and misinterpreted and is often generated by those who aren't particularly close to work either inside modern corporations or today's technology.

In terms of framing this issue for you and your organization, there are four key considerations that we find to be useful in understanding and explaining what will really happen to jobs within your industry or business.

- **Manual vs. knowledge labor:** Researchers—and many of us—still view manual labor and knowledge labor as interchangeable (and therefore "automatable" in the same way). They are not interchangeable, and therefore their substitution by machines is different.
- **Jobs vs. tasks:** We tend to look at "jobs" holistically, instead of seeing them as being composed of their various tasks, some of which can be automated and others of which will never be automated. In looking at the tasks that make up a job, we quickly see that some jobs indeed will be replaced by the machine, but others will be merely altered and enhanced.
- **Technology as job destroyer *and* creator:** Most analyses look at automation and technology solely as a job destroyer, but every major technology shift through history has also led to job creation. Dystopian

visions of the future have been largely fueled by ignoring the growth side of the equation.

- **Time:** In trying to understand the future, one of the most important variables is time. This is often overlooked or extended so far out as to make some predictions meaningless.

Let's look at these four in detail.

Manual vs. Knowledge Labor: As Goes the Factory, So Goes the Office?

For the past several decades, automation in the industrial economy has been grand in scale, yielding product improvements, process efficiencies . . . and horrid layoffs. Huge factories full of people are now more productive with 80% or 90% fewer people managing fleets of machines. Robots now make our cars, unload ships, assemble any number of products, and even vacuum our floors. When the price was right, the bots took over the work of thousands of physical laborers.

That shift was easy to see, and it was painful in a lot of ways. The three of us as authors were all raised in towns that stood as industrial leaders in the 1960s, but which had become economically depressed by the 1990s. At a human level this transition was nothing short of brutal and provided harsh truths about economics and technology. In fact, the manufacturing robot improved efficiency and boosted quality. Those jobs are gone, and they won't come back. As such, many are drawing a parallel between the blue-collar labor collapse of Detroit and a similar impending white-collar labor collapse in places like London, New York, and Los Angeles.

However, drawing such parallels has limitations, for manual labor and knowledge labor have very different attributes and, as such, the automation of them is substantially different. An old aphorism is instructive in this regard:

If I give you a dollar, then you are a dollar richer and I am a dollar poorer. But if I give you an idea we are both richer, for now we both have the idea and your reaction to it has made it more valuable to me.

Putting a lug nut on an automobile chassis, whether done by hand or machine, is done once and then there's no going back to it. Additionally, this task is the same every time it's conducted. However, knowledge automation is different, for often the atomic unit of "knowledge" can be reused many times and continually "enriched" to become more valuable over time.

As an example of this, think back to the newspapers of a generation ago. These were true one-to-many offers, as all of us received the same newsprint each morning. As such, because those knowledge products arrived in a physical form we thought of them as being similar to that lug nut.

However, now think of the *highly* personalized news feeds received online today; your local news, weather, sports scores, stock portfolio, and traffic information. All at your request, at any time or place. Think of the permutations involved in generating such customized, curated experiences. In a mid-sized city of 500,000 people, simply delivering the personalized needs across the five basic news variables (news, weather, sports, stocks, traffic) would yield 3.12^{28} permutations alone! Obviously, it's a mathematical impossibility to think that the newsroom of old could even begin to consider delivering personalized news to everybody in town. Yet today, bots, by recombining all of those units of knowledge work, can do this effortlessly (and we show how they do this in more detail in Chapter 7). Therefore, automation of knowledge assets is *not* zero-sum, in that it's not just a matter of removing existing labor. It is also allowing for more throughput, and this often manifests itself as a level of mass customization that was impossible before systems of intelligence.

This phenomenon—the codification, recombination, and repurposing—of knowledge assets has broad implications. In the coming pages, we examine how it will impact core processes in your business (within sales, human resources, supply chain management, or finance) to both streamline them and to greatly increase throughput, quality, personalization, and overall capability.

The point is, knowledge work is very different from manual labor. When the bot is applied to knowledge processes, even for the explicit purpose of automation, the underlying knowledge assets become richer and can be used (and reused) in interesting and productive ways. As such, the envelope of work potential (and corresponding output) is usually expanded, thus removing the one-to-one work substitution that occurred with the automation of manual labor.

Don't Confuse Jobs with Tasks

Related to this is the second flaw that most of the doomsday analyses share: they fail to make the crucial distinction between "jobs" and "tasks." These studies tend to view "jobs" in a binary sense (i.e., "they will be automated away" or "they will not be automated away"). That's far too simplistic; any knowledge job is a collection of tasks. Some of these tasks are ripe for automation, while others never will be. In the vast majority of cases, *portions* of a job will be impacted or replaced by the bot, while other portions of it will be untouched or even enhanced.

Consider Tamara, an accountant laboring in your company's accounting department. Her job consists of dozens of tasks, some of the primary ones being:

- Documenting financial transactions
- Preparing asset, liability, and account entries
- Preparing tax filings
- Auditing transactions and financial statements
- Recommending corporate policies and procedures
- Reconciling financial discrepancies
- Creating profit and loss statements
- Creating balance sheets
- Providing strategic counsel
- Pursuing data integrity

Some of these tasks will be automated away with the use of the new machine or made dramatically more efficient by them, but not all of them. Tamara's job will change, but it will not go away completely. To imagine that the entire profession of accounting will in short order disappear and be replaced by software is to fall prey to the trap of over-extrapolating how and how fast technology changes things in the real world.

One of the best analyses of machine-based job displacement has been undertaken by Forrester Research, which has taken the "task-based" vs. "job-based" approach. In many cases, "robotic process automation" will eliminate only *portions* of a job, most often the ones humans find to be drudgery. Thus, in many cases 20% of the routine—and highly boring—portions of a job go to the machine.

Forrester puts it like this:

The greatest change to the workforce . . . will be in job transformation—that is, occupations in which 25% or more tasks are automated, leading to redeployment and responsibility-shifting on the part of the worker. In 1992, cable TV technicians had a relatively simple job: connecting coaxial cable to a pole and into households. Since then, their job tasks have expanded to include Internet service, wireless routers for Internet, voice-over-IP (VoIP) telephony, and even home security installation. With each new task, the overall composition of the job transformed, even requiring the technician to log into your PC to activate services—a new skill set for sure. Similarly, we'll see jobs transformed across all categories . . . .[5]

Figure 3.1 highlights the percentage of job tasks that will be impacted by the machine, not necessarily replaced by the machine.

Employment Categories	2015	2016	2017	2018	2019	2020	2021	2022
Management, business, and financial	9%	19%	29%	40%	51%	64%	77%	92%
Professional and related	8%	17%	27%	37%	48%	60%	73%	87%
Protective service	6%	12%	19%	26%	35%	44%	54%	66%
Non-protective	6%	12%	19%	27%	35%	44%	55%	67%
Sales and related	7%	14%	23%	32%	41%	52%	63%	76%
Office and admin support	7%	15%	23%	32%	42%	52%	64%	76%
Farming, fishing, forestry	6%	11%	18%	24%	32%	40%	50%	62%
Construction and extraction	6%	11%	18%	24%	31%	40%	49%	60%
Installation, maintenance, and repair	6%	11%	17%	24%	31%	39%	49%	60%
Production	6%	11%	18%	24%	32%	40%	50%	61%
Transportation and material moving	6%	11%	18%	25%	32%	41%	51%	62%

Job transformations occur at two points; when the occupation's task reaches 25% cannibalization (non-net, so not including yearly CAGR job growth) and again at 50%. This forecast summarizes the years when a particular job reaches these two benchmark levels.

Source: Numbers derived from Bureau of Labor Statistics (BLS)
Used with Permission of Forrester Research, Inc.

Figure 3.1   Cumulative Percentage of Job Tasks Cannibalized (Absent Secular CAGR)

For example, the findings are not claiming that 92% of management, business, and finance jobs will disappear by 2022. Instead, they are asserting that 92% of the "workflows, processes, and metrics" in those job types will be changed by the new machine. In cases where a specific job has too many tasks "cannibalized" by AI, the job can, in fact, disappear completely. This accounts for the 12% of jobs that will be automated away.

Such a task-based analysis (by vocation) starts to paint a much more realistic picture of the machine-generated transformation of work, and it has three important elements:

- **Time:** Forrester's findings still show a significant near-term impact, but they are not suggesting the end of employment as we know it during the next few years. Also, each worker can see the steady impact of automation in his or her chosen field. Seeing the transition provides both a personal roadmap and some time to adapt or to develop new skills.
- **Eliminating rote work:** Automating 50% of a job *may not be a bad thing*. As we explore in the coming pages, in many cases this automation is focused on rote, non–value added activities (e.g., the manual grading of homework by a school teacher). When workers are liberated from such activities, how can they then reinvest their time?
- **Performance growth:** Job performance can then be enhanced. The worker can double down on the more human elements of the job, double output, or greatly increase quality of delivery. For example, automation won't make a teacher disappear; instead it can make that teacher much more effective.

Don't Overlook the Job-Growth Story

This atomic-level view of a job and its associated tasks has provided a foundation for our AHEAD model. Will some jobs be automated away by AI? Yes, of course. But far more will be enhanced, and in time millions more new jobs will be discovered, driving future employment. Our confidence in these predictions is not based just on the capability of the new machine in the present; we have seen this movie before—automation is really the story of business.

Today, we are all great beneficiaries of industrial-age automation. The creature comforts many of us enjoy—the cars we drive, the TVs we watch, the computers we use, the appliances in our kitchen, the clothes we wear, the flights we take, the food we eat, and the entertainment we enjoy—are all delivered at a price/performance ratio unimaginable just a few generations ago. After all, look no further than your 60-inch flat-screen high-definition TV, which, in real terms, costs one-third the price of the old 19-inch RCA that graced your parents' den.

All of these goods and services are the direct result of automation. However, any mention of the word "automation" in 2017 is frequently met with a negative—and sometimes viscerally negative—reaction. Many seem to forget that throughout history, automation has provided a net benefit to society. In the process of automating our work and our society, through generation after generation, three positive things have repeatedly occurred:

1. A new abundance has been created; sales of products and services produced by automation—now vastly more affordable and of higher quality—skyrocket.
2. With the new abundance, overall employment rises, even when there is less labor input per unit.
3. Society gains a net benefit, with higher living standards created by newly affordable products and services.

Each time a new form of automation is introduced, there is consternation and anxiety. After all, in the moment we often cannot yet see the new abundance, the growth of overall employment, and the net societal benefit, but we certainly recognize the initial job losses. This process of automation, initially cursed and then ultimately lauded, has repeated itself with great consistency.

Think of the steamboat, the locomotive, and the assembly line. With the introduction of each new technology, vested interests were threatened and business as usual was upended. This was the story of the aforementioned Luddites. In the context of the moment, their arguments had merit. Yet in the context of history, as we recognize how the loom clothed the world, established a foundation for global trade, initiated the growth of a large middle class, and launched various related industries, the Luddites were wrong.

Automation is a deep and unstoppable force. Automation of your core processes is a key first step for you and your organization to gain a deep operational understanding of the new machine, and to unlock its potential for future bounty. Don't allow Luddite thinking to remove those opportunities.

This may sound like the 30,000-foot theory, but it has a very practical application. As a manager, in considering automating jobs within your company, these four considerations should be useful. After all, if one is afraid to automate some internal jobs away, then, in time, *all* jobs at the company may be jeopardized (given that the company will become noncompetitive on cost). Additionally, the jobs that can potentially be enhanced by automation won't come to fruition, and new offers with their associated jobs won't come to market.

The new machine will be painful for some to accept, but this shift is inevitable; if we manage it wisely, it will ultimately be positive for our companies and our societies.

The Pace of This Transition

Our prediction is that AI will impact nearly 100% of knowledge jobs, while completely eliminating approximately 12% of them. But the key question is "When?"

AI will eat existing jobs in a "slowly, slowly, suddenly" manner. Certain tasks will quietly and increasingly become automated and will then hit a potential tipping point that will fundamentally impact the very nature of certain jobs (such as the 50% cannibalization point in the Forrester model). This transition will follow the pattern of technology adoption outlined by Bill Gates in that "We always overestimate the change that will occur in the next two years and underestimate the change that will occur in the next ten."

Consequently, it's easy to believe both sides of the job dislocation argument. In taking a short-term view (of the next three years) one can think "No way our accounting department will be automated away." Yet, in understanding the capabilities of AI platforms, one can take a 15-year view and think, "No way we will have more than a handful of people processing accounts receivables by 2030."

The key for setting a realistic timeframe lies in (a) the task-based view of work and (b) the value of the remaining human element. In looking at these two variables we can start to make solid predictions as to how quickly the bot will eat a certain profession.

Getting AHEAD in a Time of Churn

In concluding this examination of the job-destroying nature of the new machine, the perspective we've outlined provides a basis for the remainder of this book. In the coming chapters we explore the practical applications of these dynamics and what they will mean for you and your organization. In Chapter 7 we examine automation in depth, looking at specific processes, functions, and jobs within your company that are particularly ripe to be taken over by the new machine. In reading this chapter, you may think, "Hmm, Tamara in accounting is in trouble if she doesn't respond quickly." In Chapter 9 we outline the jobs that will be protected and enhanced. In Chapters 10 and 11 we look to net-new job creation through the new abundance and a process of invention and discovery.

However, before we get to determining the future of work, we need to take a deeper look at the new machine that's driving all of this change.

4

The New Machine

Systems of Intelligence

Perhaps you sometimes wonder the same things we do: "How can Uber instantly connect me to a car when I'm on a random street corner some 500 miles from home and then automatically bill my credit card, send me an invoice, and capture my passenger rating in seconds?" "How can I be watching a YouTube video on a mobile device while moving at 130 mph on a train?"

These two experiences, moments of "magic" that have become almost mundane, would have been impossible even a few years ago. What's surprising is that Uber and YouTube, in spite of offering dissimilar services, both run their operations on a "machine" with essentially the same components. This new machine, what we call "a system of intelligence," is rapidly becoming the cornerstone for companies that compete on knowledge. It sits at the center of Facebook, Instagram, Google, e*Trade, Betterment, and all the other examples of today's digital leaders.

Yet, for all its importance, the new machine is still largely misunderstood. Most of us actively consume the output of these systems of intelligence without slowing down to think about how such real-time, personalized, and curated experiences are actually created and delivered.

To that end, in this chapter we will explain what these new machines are—what the technology components are, how they fit together, what a good one looks like, what they mean to enterprise work, and how they will profoundly impact the future of your work.

We know; this overview may seem akin to when you were learning to drive as a teen and your uncle popped the hood on the car, and started to explain exactly how everything worked. Some of the lesson can be dry (e.g., "this is the carburetor; these are the spark plugs"), but as we now consume these systems of intelligence on a continual basis and need to build and implement them in our own companies to seize competitive advantage, a working knowledge is important.

Defining the New Machine

Let's start with a simple definition; then we'll unpack it a bit.

> A system of intelligence combines *software* (algorithms, business rules, machine-learning code, predictive analytics), *hardware* (servers, sensors, mobile devices, connectivity), *data* (contextualized and real-time), and *human input* (often judgment or questions).

This may sound like "a bunch of hardware, software, and data is combined, and then a miracle occurs." So let's touch on the three key attributes that make a system of intelligence so special:

- **Software that learns:** The software at the core of the new machine is like nothing we've seen before. For the first time in human history we have a tool that can *make itself*. With machine-learning software, these systems improve on their own over time. The system learns how to recognize patterns and how to find hidden insights in the data, all without being explicitly programmed on what to do or where to look. This is the way, for example, Uber knows how to match the right driver with the right passenger or how Facebook populates your personalized

News Feed. There are few humans at these companies figuring these things out. That would be impossible as, in the case of Facebook for example, there are more than one billion daily customer logins.[1] Instead, the machine learns about each and every one of those sessions, continually getting smarter.

- **Massive hardware processing power:** During the past several decades, we've seen the power of hardware technology increase exponentially. No other innovation in history has both improved and diffused this rapidly. Moore's Law, which finds that the number of transistors on a chip (and therefore processing power) doubles approximately every two years, persists in spite of having recently celebrated its 50th birthday. But lately, this has been turbocharged by the cloud, which enables hyper-powerful computers to be tied together. By way of comparison, a muscle car may have impressive horsepower, such as the 435 horses under the hood of a Ford Mustang GT, but you cannot glue two Mustangs together to go twice the speed. By contrast, with cloud computing one can tap into multiple computers to get blazing-fast performance. Thus, each time you use Google, Facebook, or Amazon, you are tapping into their hardware farms of connected, super-fast servers.

- **Huge amounts of data:** Data is the fuel of the new economy. Relate this fact to the taxi dispatcher example cited previously. In the good old days of, say, 2012, maybe three points of "data" about your ride would be captured: a record of your phone call requesting the cab, the handwritten notes of the dispatcher and the driver, and your payment details. (Of course, rarely if ever would these manual records be reviewed or analyzed.) Compare that with a typical Uber ride, which will capture data on your request, location, time, route taken, device used, payment and tip, driver, passenger, driver rating, and passenger rating. And then multiply that by the more than two billion rides taken (through mid 2016) via Uber.

In short, these three special features—software that learns, massive processing power, and enormous amounts of data—are combining to bring systems of intelligence to life. (As an aside, in some circles, these are now being referred to as software "platforms"; for clarity and consistency, we will refer to them as systems of intelligence). Further along in the chapter, we will outline how these pieces all fit together. Before we get there, it's useful to provide some definitions on the most controversial and misunderstood part of the machine—artificial intelligence.

Artificial Intelligence: Why a Narrow View Is Best

The term "artificial intelligence" has become so overused that it's actually causing more confusion than clarity. There are many definitions in the market, and almost all of them emphasize a comparison to humans. Such definitions—for example, Merriam-Webster's ("the capability of a machine to imitate intelligent human behavior")—immediately send many of us down the wrong path, for we start thinking, "What human intelligence can and will be imitated?" We think this is wrong.

Our definition is simpler:

> AI is an area of computer science that focuses on machines that learn.

It's that clear-cut. The anthropomorphically biased definitions of AI are wrong for two basic reasons:

1. AI that creates business results will focus on what machines do really well, rather than trying to replicate what humans already do well.
2. Humans have long ago proven themselves to be imperfect "machines" (just watch the six o'clock news). It seems a bit narcissistic that the design-point of the new machine should be that of a human.

Thus, AI is *not* about building robots that ape human form and behavior. Instead, practically applied AI represents the next generation of computer systems that, like the systems of old, are housed in air-conditioned computer rooms and accessed through networks and systems (like those apps on your smartphone) that you may not see but consume on a regular basis.

But such a definition is only the beginning. We've found it very helpful in slicing through the definitional clutter to divide AI into three subsets:[2]

1. Narrow AI
2. General AI
3. Super AI

Narrow AI, which is also referred to as "applied AI" or "weak AI," is our default definition for this book. It is important to note that all AI today—and for at least the next decade—is narrow (also termed "artificial narrow intelligence" or ANI). Such AI is purpose-built and business-focused on a specific task (e.g., driving a car, reviewing an X-ray, or tracking financial trades for fraud) within the "narrow" context of a product, service, or business process. It's what the FANG vendors utilize today in delivering their digital experiences. Thus, while it appears that the new machines can do everything, they actually focus on doing just one particular thing very well. As such, these ANI systems would be hopeless in any pursuits beyond those for which they were specifically designed (just ask your Waze GPS if that onion bagel with cream cheese fits your current diet). ANI is simply a tool, albeit a very powerful one, that provides the basis for all we will explore in the coming pages.

General AI, also referred to as "strong AI" or AGI, is what is fueling the fears of the *Singularity* crowd, and has been highlighted in the previously referenced films *Her* and *Ex Machina*.[3] Strong AI is the pursuit of a machine that has the same general intelligence as a human. For example, just as you in a span of a few moments can discuss politics, tell a joke, and then hit a golf ball 150 yards, the AGI computer will have the general intelligence to perform these activities as well.

Ben Goertzel, Chairman of the Artificial General Intelligence Society, points to the Coffee Test as a good definition for AGI. That is, "Go into an average American house and figure out how to make coffee, including identifying the coffee machine, figuring out what the buttons do, finding the coffee in the cabinet, etc."[4] This set of tasks that is seemingly easy for almost any adult to perform is currently insanely difficult for a computer. Creating AGI is a dramatically harder task than creating ANI; by most estimates we are still more than two decades away from developing such AI capabilities, if ever.

That said, it's easy to scare ourselves with general AI for two reasons, one practical and the other theoretical. On the practical front, we see examples today of narrow AI that appear to be general AI. This might be your Amazon Alexa home appliance, which passes the Turing test (of acting in a way that's indistinguishable from a human). It may *feel* as though it's moving toward AGI, but it's actually just a brilliantly elegant vocal interface to the Internet search capacity we've known for over 15 years.

On the theoretical front, computer scientists look at the human as a machine in and of itself—one with very distinct limitations. Human IQs generally range from 80 to 150, an incredibly small scope in computing terms. If AGI becomes a possibility from a software standpoint, why would we limit a machine's "intelligence" to, say, an IQ of 150? Why not 300 or 3,000 or 30,000? None of us would even begin to understand what such an IQ would be or could do, but when it's a simple matter of stringing together more servers in the cloud to add more processing power, where would this take us?

This leads to the third definition. **Super AI**, in essence, is the technical genie being let out of the bottle. In such a scenario, would humans even know how to stop such a machine? It would run circles around our collective intellect (and, as we know, whenever 10 reasonably smart people are put in a room, the collective IQ is not 1,200 but actually somewhere around 95 once one accounts for the different opinions and objectives that people always bring). How could we then turn the machine off when it's always 10 (or 1,000) steps ahead of us?

This is interesting stuff, particularly for cocktail party conversations. Yet, to reiterate, based on our research, a post-*Singularity* future with super AI-based Terminators running amok is a mirage. Serious people— the people building these systems today—are quite modest about whether such scenarios are even possible in the next 100 years, much less in the next 5 to 10. Andrew Ng, the chief scientist at Baidu Research, put it succinctly when he said that "worrying about [general or super] AI is like worrying about overpopulation on Mars before we've even set foot on it."[5]

Thus, our focus in this book is specifically on ANI because here, in the real world, we are more concerned about effective tool use for good business outcomes in the modern enterprise. Although some will continue fretting away, worrying about such things as super AI, their competitors will put them out of business with practical applications of narrow AI. With that as a definition of AI, let's go deeper into the new machine.

Meet the Machine: Anatomy of a System of Intelligence

Each system of intelligence can do vastly different things, but they all share a similar basic anatomy. In fact, if you are familiar with enterprise technology and the prior generation of systems of record (such as ERP and CRM systems), many of the constituent parts will seem familiar. After all, the technology "stacks" of systems of record and systems of intelligence share many common elements, such as user interfaces, application logic, process flows, databases, and infrastructure.

However, critical differences exist up and down each layer of the stack, the most important focusing on the three distinguishing characteristics of the new machine highlighted earlier: systems that learn, massive processing power, and huge amounts of data. In Figure 4.1 we highlight several of the key differences at each layer of the software stack. Next, we'll work top-down through the various components common to every system of intelligence as shown in Figure 4.2.

KEY ATTRIBUTE	SYSTEM OF RECORD	SYSTEM OF INTELLIGENCE
USERS	Internal employees.	Everybody and everything.
INTERFACE	PC-based, menu-driven. Formal "user acceptance training" required.	Any device, highly engaging and intuitive. No training required.
APPLICATION	One-to-many. The users learn the system.	One-to-one. The system learns the user.
PROCESS	Supports the business. Horizontal, standardized processes (e.g., financials, human resources, customer service).	Runs the business—central to the product or service experience. Vertical, unique processes.
DATA	Mostly internal sources, stored as historical records.	Mostly external sources (customers, products in use). Real-time input and output. Continually—and automatically—reviewed for insights. Orders of magnitude greater amounts.
INFRASTRUCTURE	Housed in internal data centers.	Hybrid model, utilizing both internal data centers and highly elastic cloud computing resources.

Figure 4.1   Systems of Record vs. Systems of Intelligence

HUMANS AND MACHINES

A SYSTEM OF INTELLIGENCE

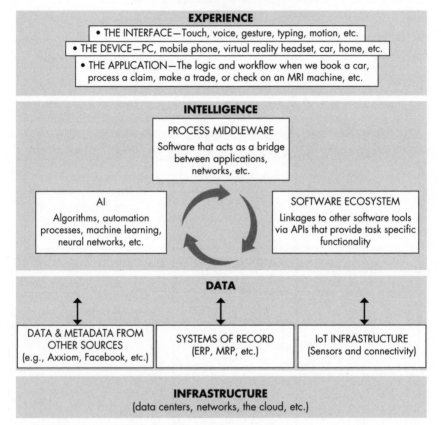

Figure 4.2   Anatomy of a System of Intelligence

Users, Customers, and Employees

Regardless of how digitized our world becomes, this shift is primarily oriented around people; that is, us—carbon-based life forms *without* an on/off switch. Thus, with successful digital solutions, the more technical they are, the more human they feel. The best digital solutions don't slow us down; instead, they get out of the way, seamlessly helping us to achieve our end goals. We don't want to learn the systems, we just want the results. With the Waze app, it's how to get somewhere by the fastest possible route; with GE's Predix platform, it's the status of our windmill farm; with the Lex Machina legal analytics service, it's the track record of a particular judge. The machines may be able to do amazing things, but the trait we've seen successful systems share is that they put the human experience at the center of the design. Oftentimes, even in the most automated, seemingly AI-rich environments, there is still a considerable amount of human intervention involved.

The App Interface

In our personal lives, we think of Netflix, Strava, LinkedIn, and so on as "apps." Most of us don't even call them "software" anymore. What you touch, the content you share, the information or insight you get—all of this flows through the app (or the application layer), which is the front door to the rest of the new machine. For years, you've downloaded apps onto your PC, your smartphone, or your tablet, and now they are being embedded into industrial machines (such as cars). What's essential here is that it's the app that frames our experience. The rest of the system of intelligence, if it's any good, is invisible to us.

Additionally, as we outlined in our book *Code Halos,* the app has to provide a beautiful experience for users. The app has to hit the FANG benchmark for elegance and ease of use. This explains the explosion of "design thinking" in corporate IT circles, given that these interfaces must fit the way in which your customers, partners, and employees wish to use them in the midst of their activities. (No owner's manuals or user training allowed!) The key to success here is that the app interface must be simple and intuitive, seamlessly fitting into the context of the user's needs.

The AI "Innards"

Beyond all the hype, ANI is modern, complex, adaptive software that is the essential core of a system of intelligence. What we think of as AI really comprises three main elements:

1. **Digital process logic:** Whenever we log onto a system of intelligence, we are engaging in a process: booking a car, processing an insurance claim, making a financial trade, or checking the status of an MRI machine. There's nothing terribly new here. An IT consultant from 1990 would recognize the technical portions managing the process flows in a system of intelligence. What is revolutionary is that systems of intelligence transform many manual processes into automated ones. Think again of the Uber versus taxi example. The car–dispatch process for a traditional taxi company is manual (e.g., customer calls in, agent informs dispatcher, dispatcher radios the appropriate cabbie, etc.). At Uber, that entire chain is automated. When that digitized process is multiplied over millions of transactions, an industry is revolutionized. We outline *how to do this* in the second half of the book. But for now, the key point is that while the technology that runs the process layer of a system of intelligence is rather simple, getting the underlying process structured properly is very hard work.

2. **Machine intelligence:** This is what's genuinely new and different about the technology of the new machine. Through a combination of algorithms, automation processes, machine learning, and neural networks, the system mimics "learning" through experience, which is really just a richer data set. This is how it can automate work processes (e.g., reading an X-ray), instruct an employee on the next best action (e.g., a salesperson knowing the precise pricing that will most likely close the next deal), and recognize market trends that will lead to the next breakthrough product. The internal "clockworks" (the software mechanism inside the system of intelligence) is machine intelligence, the true heart of AI. When viewed this way, it's not scary, arcane, or hopelessly complex. Don't get us wrong; we're not trivializing the technical complexity of creating these works. But it's not anything mystical either. For all the talk of a "ghost in the machine,"[6] in the real world, that's merely applied ANI. It's nothing more and certainly nothing less, because in the corpus of the new machine, AI is the heart.

3. **Software ecosystem:** Our apparently magical experiences with systems of intelligence may appear seamless, but we are never interacting with one piece of software. These systems are usually made up of an ecosystem of dozens of other tools connected by application programming interfaces (APIs) that are bits of software that link one tool to another like Lego blocks. Uber, for example, leverages a rich fabric of tools, including Twilio for cloud-based communications, Google for maps, Braintree for payments, SendGrid for e-mail, and so on. We each have an elegant

personal experience thanks to the Uber software interface, but we are actually engaging with an entire ecosystem of tools and services.

This is a business book for a technical age. We're not going to go into the ins and outs of the specific technologies that comprise today's artificial intelligence. We could write an entire second book on machine learning, deep learning, and neural networks (these are the hot topics in leading universities around the world), but candidly that would be redundant because there are some terrific learning resources in the market already.

Data from Things and Systems of Record

The inputs to the new machine are many and varied. Some will be mature, ERP-based systems; some will be real-time data pouring in from instrumentation—the Code Halos of data surrounding products, people, and places—that is continually informing this nerve center as to what is going on all around it. Over time, these inputs will evolve, sometimes both quickly and radically. All those inputs are responsible for creating that contextualized, highly valuable data. Without those new data sources, it will be difficult to build or fuel your new machines. Sensors in mobile devices, apparel, sporting equipment, cars, roads, and virtually every other physical entity will be responsible for generating the information—the code. Connecting those sensors to a system of intelligence is the Internet of Things coming to life.

Data may seem like a weightless abstraction. (If you're interested, all the electrons in the Internet together apparently weigh about as much as two strawberries.)[7] So while it doesn't weigh much, data has a huge amount of value when it's deployed in the right place at the right time. Massive amounts of data must be captured, stored, maintained, analyzed, and made accessible. That's why we need large database systems that that are stable, scalable, and tested (no matter how cool the shiny new tools may seem). A new generation of databases (e.g., Hadoop) are finding favor, but Oracle and SAP, with a combined customer base of more than 740,000 companies, are not going anywhere. Neither are IBM, Microsoft, or any of the other major enterprise software "arms dealers." In the digital economy, we'll still need high-quality systems of record (both traditional and emerging ones) as much as we need our AC power grid.

Infrastructure

As with any machine on a factory shop floor, the new machine needs power and "plumbing." Infrastructure includes all the networking, servers, power sources, and so forth that make the machine hum. For existing systems, many of the elements are already managed either directly by the IT department, by an external service provider, or—more common now—by a cloud provider. Mobile networking, generally running on a major carrier, is imperative. For computing power, regardless of whether your system is running on Amazon's servers, somewhere in the Google-plex, or in your own data center, systems of intelligence all need highly efficient, always-on plumbing.

Systems of Intelligence in Action

The "anatomy" of the new machine can seem somewhat abstract unless the parts are linked together into *actual* new machines visible in the real world that we conceptually understand. Much has already been said about Netflix, but our take is different. Because we are all familiar with the media-streaming platform, it provides a great illustration of how a company that is leveraging the new machine, the new raw materials, and a business model oriented around them is upending business as usual.

The Machine That Is Netflix (Thanks to AI)

As of 2016, Netflix represented about 35% of all Internet traffic in North America and has the incumbent TV networks in quite a spin.[8] By dissecting Netflix a bit, we can see the anatomy of the new machine in action. (See Figure 4.3.)

Figure 4.3   The Anatomy of the Netflix System of Intelligence

Anatomy Element	How It Works
Users/Customers	This is all of us as consumers. Netflix now has about 75 million subscribers worldwide (and growing), and we all want what we want (and we want it now, on every device, always).[9]
The App	Most of us experience Netflix as an app. Regardless of where we are or the hardware we use—tablet, mobile device, laptop, set-top box, or VR headset—the only part of the Netflix system of engagement we touch is the app that connects us to *Orange Is the New Black* (and many more).
Process Logic	Do you remember using the print *TV Guide* to find out what was on television and then having to time your life around when a show was airing? Um, neither do we. In those bygone days, there was really only one process for consuming media via television or movie screen, and it wasn't great. Now, of course, whether we are watching on a mobile device on the road or next to our loved ones at home, Netflix provides content in an almost infinite set of variations. It seems so simple now. Of course we can watch *House of Cards* at any time on a train going 130 mph! But it feels seamless and frictionless because Netflix has thoughtfully adapted its entire system to the way we want to consume content.
Machine Learning	Netflix's recommendation engine—basically, a set of algorithms that connect us to content we want—is the most well-known element of the Netflix AI system, but the whole engine is actually much more than that.[10] The core of the Netflix experience connects us to content, distinguishes between family members, and processes billions of events a day related to movies, viewers, payments, and the like. More important, the platform improves over time.

(continued)

Figure 4.3   The Anatomy of the Netflix System of Intelligence
(*continued*)

Anatomy Element	How It Works
	As we use it more, it learns about our tastes and serves up the best content available in a highly personalized way. It can distinguish between what we say we like and what we actually like. (Note, for example, that Adam Sandler's *The Ridiculous Six* is rated a middling three stars by Netflix users, but in January 2016 was the most watched Netflix program in history.)[11] The core of the Netflix system is a remarkable piece of software design and engineering, which, because it is so good, is nearly invisible.
Software Ecosystem	Netflix relies on connections to dozens of other systems to bring us *Orphan Black* and *The Walking Dead* (two of the most binge-watched shows).[12] The Netflix team emphasizes open-source software tools such as Java, MySQL, Hadoop, and others. Content distribution is supported by tools like Akamai, Limelight, and Level 3 Communications. It also relies heavily on Amazon's cloud systems for storage.[13] The point here is not the specific tools Netflix uses but that the company realized early on that it would need to build certain elements of its overall system and that it also could leverage other best-in-class systems to grow faster.
Sensors/Internet of Things	Netflix engages with us—both providing content and collecting data—via our devices, but it also learns about us via the many sensors and data associated with these devices. Other sensors are starting to matter to Netflix. For example, it is exploring ways to connect to Fitbits and even socks to monitor if we've fallen asleep.[14]
Data	The Netflix data warehouse stores about 10 petabytes of information.[15] (One petabyte is equivalent to 13.3

Anatomy Element	How It Works
	years of streaming HD-TV video.[16]) With all that data flowing through the AI engine, Netflix *knows* you. We're sorry if that creeps you out, but it tracks the movies we watch, our searches, ratings, when we watch, where we watch, what devices we use, and more.[17] In addition to machine data, Netflix algorithms churn through massive amounts of movie data that is derived from large groups of trained movie taggers. (Netflix isn't saying, but the best guess is that it is applying more than 76,000 genres to categorize movies and TV shows.[18])
Systems of Record	There's no way to manage the vast reams of Netflix data without an absolutely top-notch architecture. Netflix started with Oracle, but has moved over to an open-source database called Cassandra. It uses Hadoop for data processing and Amazon S3 for storage.[19] It also links to back-end payment systems so nothing can interfere with our next purchase.
Infrastructure	Amazon inside! As of February 2016, all of the infrastructure services Netflix requires are provided by Amazon Web Services.[20] (Anyone still waiting for the cloud to "mature" is probably tripping over the stretchy cord on his or her phone at this point.)

What Does "Good" Look Like? Attributes of a Successful System of Intelligence

There's a big difference between merely having all the necessary ingredients of the new machines and actually getting them to perform at a high level. A system of intelligence that can help you be the Usain Bolt of whatever race you're in will have all or most of these characteristics:

- **Smart, not dumb:** Effective new machines get better—more powerful and valuable—as they scale. One true test of good AI is that as data flows in, it's smarter tomorrow than today. In every case, the best systems of intelligence suck up data from a wide variety of sources, which helps achieve the data mass required to derive insights and create personalized experiences. Today's digital masters recognize that ultimately, "it's all about the data."

- **Open, not closed:** Systems of intelligence that achieve their full potential are generally more open than closed. Think of Tesla giving away its patents and Uber with its open APIs; both of these policies have helped generate new solutions built on the companies' AI cogs and gears. One of the most striking current examples of this is the competition between Amazon and Walmart.com. In many respects, using the system anatomy we have outlined in this chapter, the two look quite similar. And the customer experience through their respective apps is, give or take 10%, pretty much the same. Yet viewed through the lens of APIs, the companies couldn't look more different. Amazon has more than 325 API mash-ups that open up its platform to others. Walmart, Target, Macy's, and Sears all had three or fewer as of September 2015.[21] Openness is necessary for digital success, because a fully fleshed-out ecosystem will be more powerful than a closed development environment.

- **Smart hands, not just bots:** Most successful ANI systems include people. One of the most common mistakes that we've observed on our travels occurs when companies try to completely dispense with the human element.[22] There are lots of things that machines simply cannot do as well as we can (at least within the timeframe of a meaningful business decision). Game-changing systems of intelligence are built around the integration of AI with humans by combining the best of what computers do with the best of what humans do. (More about AI "enhancement" is provided in Chapter 9.) Some AI experiments, such as the robot hotel concierge, which attempt to mimic what humans do uniquely well, are a surefire way to waste time and money.

- **Narrow, not broad:** Trying to create one magic black box to solve all of the challenges you want AI to address might be enticing, but it's incredibly difficult to pull off. Even complex platforms like IBM's Watson or GE's Predix offer significant business value only when they are configured for a specific process or customer experience.[23] Focusing on a "moment" or a simple activity is one of the best indicators that a system of intelligence might have meaningful impact.

- **One-to-one, not one-to-many:** If you have ever worked with PeopleSoft or in an SAP environment, you know first hand that your user experience there was *not* designed for you personally. It was designed for the largest scale possible. This has been part of the architecture of almost every commercial software system since the punch card. While most existing enterprise systems are generally not designed to give us an individualized experience, systems of intelligence most definitely are. Alexa, for example, self-configures to your patterns. Amazon tunes its offerings to your virtual self. Old-school software requires you to conform to it; new-machine-age software conforms to you.

- **Bespoke, not "off the rack":** It would be nice if we could access an iTunes store offering a range of systems of intelligence and pick up solutions there for our own organizations, but that capability doesn't exist yet. Over time, AI will become "productized"—and there are many machine-learning solutions that can be accessed on an "as-a-service" basis—but for the near future, you shouldn't imagine that your organization can simply buy a complete piece of software that will instantly get you into the heart of the new machine age. New systems of intelligence are emerging every day, so things are changing fast. This is *the* biggest area for innovation across virtually every industry. If you are looking for platforms aligned to claims processing, finance and accounting processes, or secondary education classes, you are in luck, because powerful systems already exist. However, in many if not most cases, there is not yet an existing product. You should keep a sharp eye out for new solutions that will matter to your business, but for now, many of these systems must be created or assembled from existing components.

Three Key Learnings on Building Systems of Intelligence

Born from the LexisNexis® history of deep data analysis, LexisNexis Risk Solutions helps customers assess, predict, and manage risk across multiple industries (including insurance, banking, retail, health care, communications, and public sector).

Dr. Flavio Villanustre, vice president of Technology Infrastructure and Product Development, and David Glowacki, vice president of Product Engineering, are responsible for platform strategy and new product development. They are involved in a number of projects involving big data, analytics, and machine learning, and are responsible for the teams that build and run machines that are starting to do (nearly) everything.

They have created not just one, but multiple systems of intelligence that help customers manage compliance, fraud detection, health outcomes, risk, and many other core business processes. In doing so, they've gained wisdom that you can apply in your own business.

Data without a system of intelligence is just white noise. Many companies we work with are still struggling to make sense of their new raw material. Leaders are buried not only by their data; they're also buried by so many tool options—API libraries, online machine-to-machine-learning software, cloud-based solutions, automated systems, and so on. While having so many tools and capabilities widely available is a good thing, it can also be overwhelming to have so many options.

Systems of intelligence—like the ones built by LexisNexis—come to life when they connect data to a recognized meaningful outcome. As Villanustre noted, "The goal is to take an intractable problem, something that's infinitely too complex for human beings to figure out, and reduce it down to a set of data points that we can present to somebody like an investigator or an FBI analyst and derive enough information to really dive into it and kick start an investigation, if they think it's warranted."

Villanustre continued, "Leaders are coming to a greater realization: No matter what kind of data they collect—through economic transactions and other data collected within the course of their business—all data has some value. By adding a data set to another data set, you can potentially make a completely new thing."

Don't think you have to build it all yourself. As mentioned, today many system-of–intelligence solutions are simply not available "off the rack." This is where companies such as LexisNexis and others come in. "We strongly believe that the future is going to center around enabling tools," Villanustre said. "Being able to take all of the vast assets we have and present them in a meaningful way to users who may have extreme domain knowledge, but may not have any technical knowledge, is . . . broadening the number of individuals who can actually mine and take advantage of the assets that we have."

The recommendation for leaders here is to focus on the specific process or experience you want to make a system of intelligence. Once you've identified the process or experience where you want to apply new machines, investigate to see whether there is a readily available solution from a partner (such as LexisNexis). While it may be the right decision to buy piece parts of a service from a general platform provider (e.g., Google, Amazon Web Services, Palantir, Microsoft, etc.), be prepared for a substantial configuration process to make the technology fit your business requirements.

If your system of intelligence is good, you won't need 10,000 data scientists. When your systems are instrumented, you have a data flood. The conventional reflex is that companies should hire a busload of data scientists to make sense of the information. That may be a reasonable initial answer, but over time this becomes impossible to sustain.

Glowacki and his team clearly recognize that the burden of making sense of the data must shift from users to the platform. "Over time, just getting access to a mountain of data doesn't help." This is where the system of intelligence proves critical because the actual "meaning making" can be and should be encoded into the AI.

As Villanustre shared, "Why is it so hard to find data scientists today? It is because you are trying to find a unicorn. You're trying to find someone with good programming skills that also has good, deep mathematical knowledge combined with physical knowledge, as well as a good engineer with an analytical mind to break down problems and build programs. This data scientist needs to be a subject-matter expert because he or she needs to understand what they're trying to build as well as the data. We are talking about someone that doesn't exist. . . . The one thing that you can't replace is the subject-matter expert. Everything else can be built into a machine."

From Vapor to Value

In looking in more detail at systems of intelligence, many profound, strategic, even existential questions are raised. What is a department store in an age of Amazon? What is a hotel in an age of Airbnb? What is car insurance in an age of self-driving cars?

Given just how large these questions are, it's tempting to think what we are calling a major trend is actually just a fad or the latest consulting theory. We hear it all the time: Maybe this is tomorrow's problem. Maybe we should wait until regulation or a disruptive event forces change on our industry.

We disagree. Every day that passes gives us more evidence and strengthens our conviction that the new machines that we've examined in this chapter are the engines of a Fourth Industrial Revolution. We are well past the theoretical phase. Individuals and companies that are realizing an early advantage are not all geniuses or legendary entrepreneurs. They are people like you, people who are using new technologies to solve major problems.

Remember, building your own new machine is becoming increasingly easy, even though, as we have pointed out, "some assembly is still required." Increasingly you can take your credit card out and lease access to machine-learning code, infrastructure, and databases. The Google Cloud Platform gives you immediate access to a neural-net machine-learning platform.[24] Amazon Machine Learning gives you access to the same predictive analytics platform that provides recommendations to deep-pocket consultants and enterprises.[25] Only a few years ago, this would have cost companies millions and have taken many months to put into place.

The actual builders of the new machines all say the same thing: Making narrow AI the core of a system of intelligence is not a theoretical exercise; it's possible, and it's happening today. And what's really supercharging this explosion of activity is that the fuel for the new machines is all around us if you can see it, grab it, and use it, which is the focus of the next chapter.

5 | Your New Raw Materials

Data Is Better than Oil

Each industrial revolution was catalyzed by a new raw material: coal, steel, oil, electricity. This time around, data is the primary raw material.

In this revolution, the organizations that are winning know precisely how Engine T17BBI is performing *during* Flight V26 from New York to London. They know how a potential 0.5% interest rate increase in New Zealand will impact a California state government–issued zero-coupon bond *before lunchtime*. They know how a kid is performing in *today's* lesson on differential calculus. How do they know? Because they have the data.

Like oil, data needs to be "mined," "refined," and "distributed." But unlike oil, data is a multifaceted, curious commodity. It is a potentially infinite resource—opaque, ephemeral, at times intangible. It can grow quickly in scale and value, but it can also be worthless, even a burden, if it's not viewed through the right lens and managed in the right way. Today's leaders need to understand how to take this commodity, which is available to each and every one of us, and turn it into a competitive advantage. After all, harnessing the new machines without abundant data is akin to owning a fleet of tractor-trailer trucks without any access to gas.

The data we are talking about is currently under your nose, capable of being mined from your own daily business operations. For example, per our reference to Flight V26, a typical Airbus A350 has approximately 6,000 sensors across the entire plane, generating 2.5 terabytes of data *per day*.[1] And a terabyte? That's one trillion bytes, or a million million bytes. (And, yes, it's true that the word "tera" is derived from the Greek word for "monster.")

So how big is this monster data? Let's put it this way: The complete works of Shakespeare, in basic text and stored on your computer, would consume approximately five megabytes.[2] Given that a gigabyte is 1,024 megabytes, and a terabyte is another 1,024 gigabytes, it means the average A350 is producing the equivalent of 524,000 times the Bard's life's work every 24 hours. We know, you may be thinking, "What could Airbus and its airline customers possibly do with all that data? Isn't it much ado about nothing?" (Sorry, too easy.) Sometimes it is. Many organizations often don't know what to do with such data. Sometimes it's just static, and sometimes it becomes a liability. Yet in the next decade, the breakout companies will be those that become masters in consistently turning this abundant data into actionable, and proprietary, insight.

Turning Data from a Liability into an Asset

In recent years, the phrase "data is the new oil" has become something of a cliché. But like many clichés, the phrase holds an important truth. Let's unpack what it really means.

Imagine yourself in a city in the UK sometime during the 1850s—a world grimly described by Charles Dickens. The Second Industrial Revolution was well underway, and a lot of it wasn't very pretty. It was a time before child labor laws. The buildings were covered with soot. The streets were full of horses and the products of hundreds of thousands of equine digestive tracts. Many countries were in political upheaval (or worse). Unless, *m'lord,* you were at the very top of the economic food chain, life could be pretty tough and confusing.

Coal and steam still powered the economy. Oil was primarily used for lighting, waterproofing, and other incidental purposes. People knew about oil, and they did have uses for it, but nobody really saw it as the fuel for the full blaze of the Third Industrial Revolution. At that time, oil seeped through the ground or was found by miners going after coal. Oil was still seen almost as a problem—brown sticky "muck" getting in the way of mining out the coal.

In 1847, a Scottish chemist named James Young reconceptualized the understanding of oil. Having come across a natural oil seepage at a mine in Derbyshire, he applied a distillation process to efficiently convert the "muck" into something completely different and more useful—refined oil. In the years and decades that followed, more and more ideas of how to use the new commodity emerged, and the seeds were sown for the incredible boom of the oil industry, as well as every derivative industry that followed during the next 100 years.

Today, many of the hundreds of business decision makers we work with are struggling with a similar reconceptualization of their data. We have yet to come across anyone who says, "We have complete control of all our data, fully understand its value, and are hungry for more. Bring it on!" On the contrary, we hear lament after lament about the cost, complexity, and unrealized value they feel is locked in a morass of structured and unstructured data. If you ask almost any business leader of a major industrial enterprise, they'll say they see their data more as muck than as oil.

These sentiments are well captured by renowned business and technology consultant Geoffrey Moore (author of *Crossing the Chasm*, among many other highly influential books), who stated that "[data] is a liability before it's an asset."[3]

OIL	DATA
Value is linear. If 1 barrel is \$60, 10 barrels are \$600.	Value is exponential. 1 TB is worth 1X. 10 TB is $10X^2$. 100 TB is worth $100X^n$.
Mining is localized (and expensive).	Creation and capture is distributed (and can be cheap).
Distribution requires pipes and ships (always expensive).	Distribution requires a cable or cell tower (a one-time expense).
A finite commodity.	An infinite and self-generating resource (more like sunlight than oil).

Figure 5.1 Properties of Oil vs. Data

Yet, by contrast, the management teams of today's digital leaders are "data-first," focused not on product or process, but on their new raw material. Their data isn't "muck"—it's the lifeblood of the new machine, the fuel that moves it forward. In sticking with our oil metaphor, data is superior to oil as a raw material in several ways as shown in Figure 5.1.

Managing the Data Supply Chain

Turning data into actionable insight will occur not by accident but by establishing and managing a "data supply chain" across the business. This also has parallels to today's energy industry.

Oil companies are organized around three key activities: exploration and extraction, refining, and distribution; these are commonly referred to as upstream, midstream, and downstream. Oil executives have long recognized that all three of these areas are quite distinct and require different skill sets, technologies, and business-model approaches. Very few executives responsible for handling data have put in place a similar clearly delineated approach. They should. Figure 5.2 outlines this comparative concept further.

There are several important ways in which data is far superior to oil:

- **Cheap to "mine":** As the world becomes increasingly instrumented, it becomes easier and easier to create and capture data. Once you instrument an MRI machine, for example, the cost of data over time drops to nearly nothing. This is in contrast with oil. If you drill one big well, the second one isn't much cheaper.
- **Infinite and shared:** There have been warnings about "peak oil" (i.e., running out of it) from almost the moment James Young started selling people on the idea of its value. To this day, no one really knows how much oil there is, but it is certain that we aren't getting any more, and without technology advancing, it's becoming harder to access.[4] Data, your new raw material, isn't found deep in the ground somewhere on the other side of the world. Instead, it's under your feet and under your nose right now; you just have to grab it. And unlike coal or oil, which are "zero-sum," data and insight actually increase in value the more you use them. After all, adding one drop of oil to another simply yields two drops. However, combining one piece of data from your operations with another from a customer or a business partner could yield huge benefits.

OIL	DATA
UPSTREAM	**EXPLORATION** (seismic, rock, basin, analysis, etc.) **DRILLING** (wells, rigs, platforms, etc.) **PIPELINE INFRASTRUCTURE**	**INSTRUMENTATION** (distributed control systems) **SENSORS** (LIDAR, auxanometer, IPv6, etc.) **DATA CAPTURE SOFTWARE** (for both physical devices and software-based systems) **CONNECTIVITY** (RFID, NFC, Bluetooth, ZigBee, LiFi, etc.)
MIDSTREAM	**REFINING** (processing plants, oil depots) **STORAGE TANKS**	**DATABASES** (Hadoop, Hana, NoSQL, etc.) **ALGORITHMS** (third-party, i.e., Amazon RDS, and proprietary) **LOGICAL MODELS** (business and technical)
DOWNSTREAM	**RETAIL SERVICE STATIONS** (processing plants, oil depots) **PRODUCT DISTRIBUTION** (trucks, ships, rail, etc.)	**DEVICES** (phones, health wearables, smart home networks, etc.) **USER INTERFACE** (presentation layer) **USER APPLICATIONS** **COMMERCIAL OPTIMIZATION**

Figure 5.2   The Supply Chains of Oil vs. Data

- **Proprietary in nature:** Oil is, by definition, a commodity. What is produced in Alaska, Nigeria, or Saudi Arabia is essentially the same—and is valued as such on the open market. Your data, on the other hand, is proprietary. It's unique, and it trades, if you will, in a closed market. If managed properly, this provides it with immense value. Such proprietary data, at scale, is the moat that exists around the franchises of Google, Facebook, and Uber; in the coming years, your proprietary data will become the competitive moat around your business. As a bank, it's how you will assess risk in ways your competitors cannot. As an insurer, it will be how you revolutionize the actuarial science. As a health care provider, it will be how you fundamentally transform patient outcomes and reset your cost base.

- **Cheap to distribute:** The Trans-Alaska Pipeline System cost about $8 billion to build; its owners continually wrestle with the huge maintenance costs. Access to data is really expensive initially—building and maintaining cellular networks is neither free nor cheap—but the value of the information being shipped (movies, music, car telematics data, robo-journalism articles, cat pictures) can increase enormously without a corresponding increase in distribution costs. Moving 75,000 barrels of oil an hour takes a pipeline of a certain size; no compression algorithm or switch upgrade can condense that volume.

- **Exponentially valuable:** The value of oil is like that of any other commodity. The price of a barrel is set by the market, and each barrel at any time costs about the same. It's a linear relationship between value and volume. Data, however, conforms to a different model. It follows more of an exponential curve. A little bit of the right data might be worth something, but perhaps not much. Once there's enough data to draw more valuable conclusions, though, the value of the data set increases exponentially. Netflix wouldn't know much about us if only 10 people used it. Google wouldn't work either without billions of searches. The real value of code is that once you have enough data, the value goes through the roof.

This three-pronged approach—upstream, midstream, and downstream—is a useful way of thinking about organizing your technology, staffing, and approach to building your own new machine.

Business Analytics: Turning Data into Meaning

In time, we believe the structure we have described of harvesting, refining, and distributing data will become a universal practice. Data harvesting will become standardized and, thus, "table stakes." By 2020, Ford will not seize any advantage over Chevrolet by instrumenting the car's carburetor. Similarly, the distribution of information via apps and embedded systems will become a commodity. After all, the success of Google vs. Bing or Amazon vs. Walmart.com has almost nothing to do with the distribution and interface, because in each case they are largely the same. However, the middle step, the refining of data or turning it into meaning, will be the key competitive battleground. This is where competitive distinction can be created and maintained. This is where you and your teams will need to *convert* the data into insight and *apply* that insight via new commercial models; and this is where business analytics comes into the frame.

Business analytics can be defined as the tools, techniques, goals, analytics, processes, and business strategies used to transform data into actionable insights for business problem solving and competitive advantage.[5] In our research at Cognizant's Center for the Future of Work, we have determined that a company that harnesses value from data better than its competitors can enjoy an average cost decrease of about 8.1% and an average revenue increase of about 8.4%.[6]

Before you can order your analysts to analyze, though, you need to give them something to analyze; this is where turning everything—really everything—into a "code generator" comes into the picture.

If It Costs More than $5, and You Can't Eat It, Instrument It!

Smartphone vs. dumb phone. Remember the dumb phone? The black or beige block of plastic with a rotary dial that sat in your parents' living room? OK, sometime in the 1980s, it gained a punch-dial keypad, but it was still dumb, completely incapable of storing numbers, tracking calls, or anything like that.

Why do we bring up vintage phones? Well, the way we view the dumb phone now is how we will view today's walls, desks, glasses, shoes, cars, toothbrushes, forks, houses, fridges, elevators, doors, trains, televisions, pacemakers, hearing aids, credit cards, ticket booths, lights, sports stadiums, plane seats, restaurants, factories, roads, subways, offices, museums, and so on by 2025. Dumb. Amazed that they couldn't adapt to our needs in real time and that they couldn't help us in our tasks, providing new insight and context, in real-time. As such, we are on the verge of the smart-product transformation.

At the heart of this transformation is the instrumentation of everything; as sensors have become miniaturized and their price/performance curve has become "Moore-ish," it has become possible, technologically and economically, to put them into smaller and smaller objects.[7] Not just possible but imperative. After all, to know everything about everything, you need to instrument everything. The strategic question shouldn't be "What should we instrument?" but rather "What *shouldn't* we instrument?" as not instrumenting something should be the exception, not the norm. And, in doing so, not only will you begin the process of harvesting all the data in your organization, but you will also greatly increase the intrinsic value of the very objects you are instrumenting.

Table for Two? Or Two Thousand?

Take this one simple example: a non-sensor-enabled table that costs $150 to make might retail at around $500. A sensor-enabled table that costs $200 to make could potentially retail at $1,000. Consider a "smart" table that could adjust its height automatically for different users (the way a car seat does), charge electronic devices with no need for charging cables, allow someone to type or draw on it directly and then project those commands onto a digital whiteboard, display the name of the person sitting at the table, or track whether someone was sitting at it (or not) and adjust surrounding heating and lighting conditions accordingly. Any of these possible scenarios would be hugely more valuable to purchasers. For a relatively modest increase in manufacturing cost, an incredible opportunity for increasing revenue and profitability would be unleashed. And then, think through the "stickiness" of the smart table. A dumb table can be swapped out for another with no problem. However, doing the same with the smart table would result in a sudden removal of the personalization that surrounds it. The lights in the room wouldn't work the same, for example, or the digital whiteboard would sit dark. The history of that worker's preferences would be lost. Suddenly, that table becomes very "sticky" for its users.

If you take this one mundane example of something "dumb" becoming "smart" and extrapolate it into the "universe of things," the impact of instrumentation becomes more and more profound. This is how and why GE is making its industrial windmills "smart"; this is how and why Bosch and Samsung are making their consumer white goods (i.e., fridges and ovens) "smart." It's also why there's an explosion of activity around the idea of instrumenting *people*. Let's face it; at times we're pretty "dumb" too. Instrumenting *us* will help us get smarter about a lot of important things, like our health, as well.

The Home–Field Advantage of Big Companies

So if every "thing" needs to be instrumented, the question is raised: Who has most of these "things?" The answer: the typical 100-year-old company.

The Silicon Valley elite and the software unicorns[8] don't have these assets that are soon to be transformed from dumb to smart. It's the hospital that has the beds, the operating rooms, and the intensive care units, all waiting to be instrumented. It's also the hospital that has the patients in its care, all needing to be tracked. This is not the case for some faraway, venture-backed software start-up.

We find too many traditional companies saying they feel insecure in the burgeoning digital economy, claiming they are burdened with inherent disadvantages (in legacy systems and processes, cost structures, physical assets, facilities, culture, etc.). This may be so. But they also come armed with a fundamental and massive advantage: they now own all the new data generators, the "things" of their operations, and their customers. This is an advantage not to be relinquished, and it must be protected through an instrumentation imperative.

First Data Is Now in First—with Data

Another long-established company reimagining its product portfolio is one you probably interact with every day. First Data, based in Atlanta, Georgia, manufactures the point-of-sale (POS) devices you encounter when you swipe your credit or debit card or scan your mobile device at the pharmacies, grocery stores, or restaurants you frequent. In addition, the company manages the entire back-end payments process—after the card is swiped or inserted—for the six million businesses, four thousand financial institutions, and government agencies it serves, making it the world's largest merchant acquirer and issuer processor. In the U.S. alone, First Data processes nearly half of all credit and debit card transactions. Although this is an unglamorous task, it is absolutely fundamental to the enablement of commerce around the world.

With the rise of FinTech start-ups, it was important for First Data to adapt its business to keep up with both the pace of payments technology change as well as the needs of all businesses—from new entrepreneurs to major big-box retailers. In strategizing how to respond to this increasing competition, First Data understood it needed to evolve its product portfolio. After all, similar to the home telephone of old, many viewed these devices as "dumb bricks" for credit card transactions.

For decades, First Data thrived on its payment processing business, and so it wasn't completely clear whether investing further in its POS portfolio was still a good business model. Then, in 2013, Frank Bisignano became First Data's new CEO. In understanding the emerging digital economy, Bisignano recognized First Data had a massive home-field advantage: the company's position as the world's largest merchant acquirer provided significant opportunity for unparalleled distribution of its POS devices. Those "dumb bricks" had potential massive value. Bisignano understood that the relatively "dumb" POS readers could be become "smart"—similar to the smartphones consumers carry in their pockets every day. Infused with sensors, new software, and hundreds of third party apps, the POS "brick" could move beyond simple payments acceptance and instead become a comprehensive business management tool.

With this new perspective, First Data decided to reposition itself in the marketplace with a next-generation unified software and a hardware "platform" to safely and securely enable POS, business intelligence, and commerce-enhancing services. The transaction data First Data is able to collect is now allowing the company to know who is buying what, where, when, and how. As a result, the company has insights into, for example, how customer behavior and loyalty actually manifests itself in a store. First Data's POS software and hardware is known as Clover. The product line features a series of sleekly designed POS devices that double as business management tools, including an app market that serves a variety of business needs from employee time and inventory manage-ment to salon appointment booking.

Over time, First Data's Clover operating system and hardware have revolutionized how the company is viewed in the marketplace. Instead of simply providing the platform for credit card transactions, First Data can become a true partner to its retailers by offering innovative commerce technology. An example of this is all the data that is captured and transmitted by that newly smart brick, that little machine that can lead to greater insights than the store staff may recognize. First Data leaders clearly recognized the value of data, and are doubling down on their new "smart terminals." Their newest Clover payment system is actually the entry point to a platform world that allows the company to help merchants manage their supply chains and workers, offer loyalty programs, improve security, and—oh yes—collect payments.

This jujitsu move of taking a seeming disadvantage and using it as an advantage can serve as an example to all "pre-digital" companies looking to retool. The truly digital economy, full of Know-It-All businesses, could, in fact, be the era of "the revenge of the 100-year-old firm." American Express, for example, has a stockpile of data in a closed-loop system, as issuer, underwriter, and processor from customer transactions going back decades. Airlines, banks, and insurance companies (some around since Madison was president of the United States) all have valuable data ready to be extracted and refined.

That's the good news, but a significant threat still looms. One advantage that oil has over data is that it is timeless. The oil in the ground today is largely the same as it was 100 years ago, which is the same as it will be in 50 years. Though its value will fluctuate wildly due to the commercial battles fought by petro-states around the world, the oil itself won't change. However, the advantage of data-rich traditional companies is highly perishable. If this sounds a bit too dramatic, well then, just look around. The taxi business has been around for centuries, but Uber is now pooling massive amounts of data from the assets owned by others—us, its drivers, Google Maps, and so on. This data is integrated through Uber's platform, and now it is applying its new model not just to taxis but also to a host of other products and services (flu shots, puppies, food, yachts, helicopters, and much more to come).[9] Using the new raw material, Uber is playing the new game for a new commercial era.

Clever innovators are already figuring out how to grab decades' worth of data seemingly overnight. Leaders will either act to capture this data and value now, or be faced with a "sorry, and thanks for playing" result.

Data Is Job One

For the three of us in our consulting travels, we have a one-question litmus test to determine a company's digital readiness: Is the management team we're working with obsessive about data or not? We sometimes think of it as the "data point test," as in "How do we know they are serious about digital? Because they always go where the data points."

Those who are making true progress toward "being digital" have increasing faith in data; they recognize it as their source for proprietary insight and advantage, and for good reason. In our recent study of over 2,000 companies across the globe with a combined revenue of $7.3 trillion,[10] the executives surveyed estimated that fully a third of their industry revenues—$20 trillion—would soon be touched by digital.[11] That's a lot of people, things, and events acting as code generators. That's a lot of insight—$20 trillion worth.

This is truly becoming an age of knowing it all. Yet, without the right business model to support your data-fueled new machines, you won't get very far. So, let's now explore the third of the Three M's, the digital business model.

6 | Digital Business Models

Your Five Ways to Beat Silicon Valley

Silicon Valley is coming. There are hundreds of start-ups with a lot of brains and money working on various alternatives to traditional banking. The ones you read about most are in the lending business, whereby the firms can lend to individuals and small businesses very quickly and—these entities believe—effectively by using Big Data to enhance credit underwriting. They are very good at reducing the "pain points" in that they can make loans in minutes, which might take banks weeks. We are going to work hard to make our services as seamless and competitive as theirs.

Jamie Dimon,
Chairman and CEO, JPMorgan Chase,
2016 Annual Shareholder Letter

Silicon Valley is also coming for *your* company. Digital disruptors in your industry are armed with the new machine, fueled with data. As we have just outlined in the two preceding chapters, you can do the same and, if you go about it correctly, with even greater success.

That said, harnessing the power of the new machine alone is not enough. The final piece of the puzzle, and the ultimate determinant of your success, is surrounding it with the right business model.

Ten years ago, you had to learn how to compete at "the China price" as globalization mercilessly drove unit costs down. Today, your business needs to take another step-change, learning to compete at "the Google price," not to mention the "Google speed." In that pursuit, most industrial business models are currently too slow, too expensive, and too cumbersome. They crumble under their own weight in the face of digital competition.

What do we mean by "business model?" It's the process architecture and supporting organizational model through which your company competes. It's how an insurer processes a claim, a bank determines a car loan, or a retailer manages its supply chain and makes money from doing so. Today, in the vast majority of cases, these core aspects of a business are suddenly archaic.

In every well-established company, these business models and supporting processes were formed long before digital technology appeared on the scene. Back then, knowledge work could not be virtualized, aggregated, and instantly distributed to the right people in the right format. (Just think of attempting to create a Facebook equivalent a generation ago without the Internet, smartphones, or relational databases.) As such, knowledge work was structured very similarly to manual labor, and consequently, we're often left with seas of cubicles—in large rooms, in suburban office parks, under fluorescent lights—in which workers push paper to one another. At Ford Motor Company, the accounting staff of the 1930s was structured on the model of the company's River Rouge assembly line (see photos in Figures 6.1 and 6.2). The Taylorism that was born in the factory made its way into the office, with the focus primarily on the efficiency and quality of manually processing knowledge work.

While such structures all made sense at the time, we will soon look back and wonder, "Why did we do things that way?" Warren Buffett characterized it well in the context of the news business:

If Mr. Gutenberg had come up with the Internet instead of movable type back in the late 15th century and for 400 years we had used the Internet for news and all types of entertainment—and all kinds of everything else—and then I came along one day and said, "I've got this wonderful idea. We are going to chop down some trees up in Canada and ship them to a paper mill—which will cost us a fortune to run through and deliver newsprint—and then we'll ship that down to some newspaper and we'll have a whole bunch of people staying up all night writing up things, and then we'll send a bunch of kids out the next day all over town delivering this thing and we are going to really wipe out the Internet with this" . . . it ain't going to happen.[1]

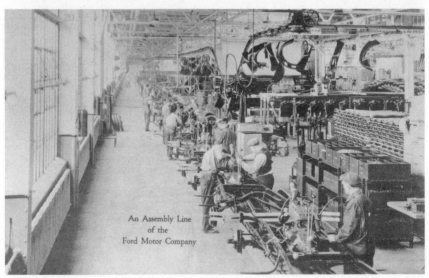

Figures 6.1 and 6.2 Knowledge Work and Physical Work Assembly Lines

Of course, such a scenario sounds absurd. Yet you will soon look back on several aspects of your business with the same incredulity that Buffett views the old newspaper business.

That skepticism is already apparent to many of your employees. Millennials, while waiting for an answer to emerge from "cube land," may often ask, in frustration, "Why can't there just be an app for this?" For a generation that has defaulted to digital, filling out mortgage forms in triplicate seems like utter madness.

In defense of many organizations, though, there are good reasons for long-standing processes to be entrenched and tough to change: quality control, institutional knowledge, fraud management, and regulation, to name a few. And, of course, the daily crush of your operations is enough to deal with—managing the supply chain, dealing with customers, processing orders, managing cash flow—making it easy to defer change for another day. Stability is to be admired, but in the digital economy such considerations can lead to stasis.

With the coming ubiquity of the new machine, however, as we have outlined in the previous chapters, stasis is no longer a viable strategy. Competitors, new and old, will not only be able to change the rules of the game from the outside by delivering vastly improved customer experiences through digital with mobile apps, instrumented products, and advanced analytics for one-to-one customer management. They will also begin changing the basis of competition from the *inside,* using the new machine to rewire core internal processes. Doing so will fundamentally change their cost base, as well as the speed of their operations and their ability to derive insight on all aspects of the business. Truly better, faster, cheaper. Very simply, in the face of the new machine, manually based knowledge processes do not stand a chance.

With that said, what do you do about it? How do you get your company to move forward? After all, a second great contributor to stasis is *too many* ideas on how to address the digital threat. We call it being "catatonic by cacophony." You've probably been in some of these meetings that soon feel like debates. Some may point to digital leaders, advising, "Let's be the Amazon of our space," while others think, "That sounds inspiring. Yet, I have no idea what it actually means."

Others argue for starting small by launching a few pilot programs. That sounds reasonable, until somebody in the room says, "Even in the best of conditions, if we extrapolate the growth of those pilots over the next three years, it won't move the needle for us." Still others may argue, "I'm tired of hearing about digital. That's for other industries, but not ours. Let's just get back to what we've always done best." Half the room then stares back in incredulity. None of it feels good, but then you go back to your daily operations until the next offsite strategy meeting. So how do you get unstuck?

Hybrid Is the New Black

Let's start by putting the right frame on the issue. Too often, the conversation on "going digital" feels binary: "the industrial firms of the past" vs. "the digital firms of the future." This is far too simplistic.

With "digital that matters," the winning business model will be hybrid—part physical, part digital. The airline of the future will still need to get the 280-ton, 300-seat Boeing 787 Dreamliner from New York to London. Yet, much of the passenger experience and flight operations— before, during, and after the flight—will be digitized. Similarly, a hospital will always have its in-person emergency room, operating rooms, intensive care units, and recovery wards, but all will become heavily instrumented and digitized. Some processes will look much the same as they do today, while others will be fully automated and unrecognizable.

As such, your challenge in building a digital business model is different from that of, say, building Twitter. You have an industrial business with existing processes, systems, and culture that has to transition to a blend, a hybrid, with just the right mix of industrial and digital. But what goes where? What stays physical, and what goes digital? And what becomes a mix of physical and digital, and to what degree? For example:

- In looking at your customer channels, what stays with your people (e.g., your sales force, retail stores, etc.) and what goes virtual? Should, for example, a retail bank actively shrink its branch network while transitioning customers to the Web and mobile apps?
- With your product portfolio, which new commercial models should be pursued? Should you begin to reclassify your products as digital services, much like Uber (car as a service), Airbnb (lodging as a

service), WeWork (space as a service), Netflix (movies as a service), Nike (personal health management as a service), and GE (industrial uptime as a service)?

- With your process portfolio, where can the new machine drive significant efficiencies? Do you start with core processes or contextual ones? How do you structure such initiatives? Do you create a "newco," essentially running two companies in parallel—or attempt to transform the current operational process (often referred to as "changing the engines while the plane is in flight")?

It's all enough to make your hair hurt. This new business model design and implementation can seem daunting. However, best practices are emerging. In our work with over 100 industrial companies looking to make this transition, in addition to our research on thousands of others, the path to business model digitization is becoming clear.

In the remainder of this chapter, we outline the path forward to building the winning hybrid model of the future. All of our work can be distilled into two big pieces of insight from all of these digital transitions:

1. Avoiding failure: The four traps to avoid in digital transformation
2. Getting AHEAD: The five ways to harness the new machine

Let's start by looking at the primary ways in which digital initiatives go bad.

Avoiding the Four Traps

In working with as many clients as we do on digital transitions, we see that the four biggest traps that even the best-intentioned executives consistently fall into with business model redesign are:

1. The "doing digital" vs. "being digital" trap
2. The FANG trap
3. The "boil-the-ocean" trap
4. The denial trap

Let's investigate each of these in more detail.

Trap 1: Taking the Easy Way Out of "Doing Digital" vs. "Being Digital"

Too often we see the superficial use of digital technology, such as putting a mobile front-end on an existing enterprise application that supports an industrial business process. It's quick, it's cheap, it's low risk. But it's also like climbing a tree to get to the moon; you will convince yourself you're making progress toward your digital goal (and, technically, you are), but you will never reach your destination.

We consistently see far too many managers taking fourth-generation machines and jamming them into third-generation business models. Then they wonder why there isn't value being created.

We refer to this phenomenon as "doing digital"—managers simply gluing digital solutions onto industrial business models. Rickard Gustafson, the CEO of Scandinavian AirLines (SAS), framed the problem well:

> For us, it's not just about putting some lipstick on a pig and trying to portray a nice portal to the customer. You need to have efficient tools. You need to have an efficient Web offering. You need to have an app. You need to connect to your customers on these mobile platforms, but the key for us is also how do you automate and digitize the inside of SAS.[2]

"Digitize the inside of SAS." Translation? Rethinking, rearchitecting, and rebuilding the supporting business model. Being digital. To gain the truly outsized results that are achievable (and that we outline throughout this book), the supporting business model has to be digital through and through, with process flows and supporting organizational structures based on digital principles instead of industrial ones.

Trap 2: The FANG Trap

Many have attempted to mimic the FANG vendors or the technology company unicorns. Intuitively, it makes sense; after all, they are today's digital masters, and we look to these players with appropriate awe. The problem is not only does this not work, but in several cases we've seen it be highly counterproductive. These firms are from different industries than yours and have different starting and end points.

An assumption contained in the question with which we opened this book ("Will we be Ubered?") is the notion of "How do we become like Uber?" In the vast majority of cases, that's the wrong question, and in fact, many times it is a dangerous question. More value has now been destroyed than created, costing time, money, and personal reputation, by firms that attempt to become "the Amazon of our space."

Why? Very simply, it's because the FANG vendors are playing a different game. They (a) are in different industries from yours, (b) had a different starting place, and (c) are targeting a different destination. They built digital businesses from the ground up, creating a purely digital company. Your challenge is different. You need to transition from being an industrial leader into leading as a digital/industrial hybrid organization. Your starting point is different; you have an industrial-era installed base of existing processes, products, and culture. Probably more important, your end goal is different. That's a different challenge from being a digital middleman like Airbnb or creating social media platforms like Facebook or Twitter.

We find blind FANG imitation as being similar to a CFO asking, "What would LeBron James do?" The basketball superstar is absolutely brilliant at breaking down a zone defense during a tense play-off game. However, he probably wouldn't be very helpful to a CFO looking to create, say, a new corporate dividend program. He's playing a different game.

That said, there are a few important areas of the FANG game you need to know cold and that *are* transferable to your business. They are:

- **The new customer expectation:** The online experiences provided by the FANG vendors are elegant, simple, and easy to use. They are highly personalized, providing custom content and curated experiences. As such, your product experiences are now being juxtaposed against the FANG expectation. It's why, for example, so many observe, "My $300 smartphone is so smart, and yet my $30,000 car is so dumb." This gap in expectation and experience will close in the coming years.
- **Trust in data:** The FANG players have corporate cultures that trust deeply in data. This may seem like a superficial issue, but it's actually profound and central to how a digital company must be run. In industrial companies, there are many different models for decision-making. For example, there's the personality-led culture (e.g., "Why did

we make that decision? Because the CEO said so!"). In some circles, this is known as HIPPO culture (i.e., *highest paid person's opinion*). Other cultures are deal-led; investment banking and Hollywood come to mind. Still others are process-oriented or regulation-led. While these factors will remain important, in the digital business, all must evolve to first holding faith in the objectivity of data and what it says about products, people, and performance.

- **Harnessing the power of the new machine:** FANG leaders are all deep believers in and implementers of AI. The CEOs of all these companies have stated, in one way or another, that their companies are "AI first." Copy that. Send your teams on "digital safaris" to Silicon Valley to, if nothing else, gain insight into the state of the art in operational AI at scale.

Trap 3: Boiling the Ocean

This third point is often the most difficult. We have recognized a best practice of keeping initial projects relatively small. Many highly ambitious management teams decide to go "all in" on digital. They rally the troops, communicate their plans to the board of directors, and confidently declare their intentions inside the company and out (you may still have some of the T-shirts and mouse pads). Then, a year or two down the line, people start asking basic questions: "How is the digital plan going? How has it changed core metrics, like sales or profits? How many customers are now on the platform?" Such questions usually induce highly uncomfortable, staring-at-shoes body language. Although well-intentioned and in many cases very well-resourced, such change initiatives don't work.

Now, this piece of advice is not one-size-fits-all. There are cases in which companies (due to industry structure or competitive moves) find themselves far behind in digital capability. In such cases a "go big or go home" approach may be necessary . . . for such a high-risk approach is warranted if a company finds itself in a laggard situation. Yet, for the 80%-plus of other companies, we advise to start small.

In starting small, find a subset of a process, one that is simple organizationally, with a straightforward digital technical application, and find quick success. Also, in starting small, build a team of like-minded digital enthusiasts. These team members will be self-selecting. As a best practice, do not try to convince anybody to join your team. If someone voices skepticism or sees the new approach as somehow too risky, move on.

Once this digital SWAT team starts to string a few victories together, momentum will build. Remember the words of Confederate General Stonewall Jackson, who during the American Civil War confounded the Union with a string of victories, in spite of inferior resources:

> *Never fight against heavy odds, if by any possible maneuvering you can hurl your own force on only a part, and that the weakest part, of your enemy and crush it. Such tactics will win every time, and a small army may thus destroy a large one . . ., and repeated victory will make it invincible.*[3]

We have found such an approach to digital business model change to be the most effective. Find discrete targets in key processes. Devote the full energies of your best business analysts and technicians to them. Then, with a series of digital successes under its collective belt, the entire organization will begin to gain confidence in the approach. Small changes can have big consequences.

Looking back at the Jamie Dimon quote that opened this chapter, you can see he noted something vitally important in digital business model generation: Digital start-ups "are very good at reducing the 'pain points' in that they can make loans in minutes, which might take banks weeks." "Reducing the pain points" is not "boiling the ocean." Dimon did not say, "reengineering the entire process"—or the entire organization. Instead, he advises finding the specific pain points that can be relieved and liberated with digital technology.

We surveyed over 300 European and U.S. business leaders to understand how and where they are applying digital tools and techniques to optimize work. As shown in Figure 6.3, we found that focusing on outdated process bottlenecks and pressure points is, by far, the best practice in helping to create healthier business outcomes and improving work experiences for customers, suppliers, partners, and employees.[4]

In that study, we found a range of ways in which companies are applying what we call "digital process acupuncture":

- Insurers are capturing images with drones to reduce insurance under-writing risk and bring them closer to real customer needs.

- Retailers are using digital wallets and beacon technologies to create shopper awareness and boost retail sales.
- Manufacturers are using sensors, the Internet of Things, and RFID for real-time monitoring to streamline the supply chain.

PERVASIVE PROCESS POTENTIAL:
ACTUAL DIGITIZATION VS. PILOTS IN FLIGHT

Percentage of business processes that have already been digitized, as well as those being piloted or considered for process digitization.

BANKING & FINANCIAL SERVICES

	CURRENTLY	PILOT	CONSIDERING
Wealth management	40%	38%	14%
Post-trade processing service development	42%	33%	23%
Front-office	47%	31%	19%
New product service development	56%	31%	9%

INSURANCE (PC&L)

	CURRENTLY	PILOT	CONSIDERING
Actuarial	44%	40%	15%
New business, underwriting & customer support	44%	33%	20%
Claims administration	51%	31%	15%
Risk, fraud, compliance	56%	25%	16%

HEALTHCARE PAYER

	CURRENTLY	PILOT	CONSIDERING
Overpayment recovery services	34%	23%	40%
Fraud & abuse services	43%	42%	9%
Member provider customer support	49%	19%	28%
Medical management	55%	28%	9%
Claims coding & processing	55%	25%	15%
Enrollment & billing services	64%	25%	6%

RETAIL

	CURRENTLY	PILOT	CONSIDERING
Back-office support processes	21%	35%	36%
Goods sourcing & supply chain	13%	35%	41%
Merchandising	21%	28%	41%
Market goods & services	12%	37%	45%
Customer & order management	14%	26%	52%
Shopping experience & channels	8%	17%	67%

Response base: 321

Source: Cognizant Center for the Future of Work.

Figure 6.3 Pervasive Process Potential: Actual Digitization vs. Pilots in Flight

When organizations identify the pressure points and apply digital solutions in very targeted ways, small changes can spark big results. Our research has found that by applying digital tools and techniques, respondents are trimming "fat" to the tune of 8% in cost reductions as well as building digital "muscle" with revenue growth of 10%. In the aggregate, digital process improvements implemented through targeted, narrow steps collectively propelled an 18% net positive for the companies we studied. Spreading this highly focused approach into the rest of the organization is critical, as it:

- Significantly boosts the impact of cost reductions.
- Speeds time-to-market improvements.
- Eliminates friction points.

We also discovered that well over half of all respondents said digital process initiatives have resulted in significant levels of process value chain integration. (We'll give more detailed guidance on where to start this type of work in Chapter 7.)

Trap 4: The Digital Denial Trap

Digital deniers like to say, "I love what Silicon Valley has provided in my personal life. And, yes, some industries have been hit hard by digital. But we won't be. Our industry is different." Such thinking is dangerous; those who voice it are in industries that haven't been fully hit by digital yet.

The digital revolution is unevenly distributed. That is, some industries, and their supporting business models (i.e., newspapers, maps, book retailing) have forever been transformed, while others (i.e., energy and utilities) are still relatively untouched.

What accounts for this? There are many factors, including industry structure, nature of the product or service, and regulatory restrictions. However, in our view, the primary factor is the amount of data that is swarming the business.

In nature, elements become unstable with significant changes in temperature and must transform to regain harmony with their environment. Similarly, many businesses have become highly unstable in this era of hyperconnectivity. Just as rising temperatures force change upon matter (with, say, ice turning to water), today's rapid rise of information is forcing structural change upon many corporate models.

Each year in New England, the changes in season turn winter's ice rink into summer's swimming pond. Whether one skates on the ice, swims in the water, or stares up at the clouds, the integrity of the water in any of its forms is never questioned. Water is water, for regardless of its state, it is always two parts hydrogen, one part oxygen. Importantly, we inherently understand the stability of each form given its environment.

There's a strong parallel between the natural states of matter and the proper, or natural, state of an organization. Just as the state of matter naturally changes with increases in temperature, the state of the organization must change with meaningful increases in information (see Figure 6.4).

Figure 6.4 Melting Points in Nature and Business

Unfortunately, many managers today are confused. They focus on the state of their organization instead of its substance. For example, management at Borders, Blockbuster, and other retailers defined their organizations as physical retailers that happened to sell books or rent videos, instead of as book and video providers that needed to take on the appropriate form for their market context. Incorrectly conceptualizing the business proved deadly in those markets.

If your industry isn't yet addressing this structural challenge, it's because your sector, like a substance in nature, simply has a different "melting point." It's why so many managers, yet to be hit by this technology wave, make statements like "That's a music or book thing, but our industry is different." And yet, the only difference is the industry's melting point. For example, water melts at 32° Fahrenheit, but aluminum melts at 1,221° and tin at just 449°. Just as no substance is immune to heat, no industry structure is immune to today's explosion of information.

Thus far in this chapter we've outlined the four big digital initiative killers. Now let's turn to a more optimistic perspective to highlight the five approaches for building winning digital business models.

Five Ways to Mine Gold from the New Machines

For companies working to get AHEAD, there isn't just one form of business model transformation; there are five. A quick summary of each follows, and as you prepare for the second half of the book (which is much more implementation-oriented and where we go into much more detail about each of these areas), think through which portions of your operations or potential digital initiatives fit into which category.

- **Automate:** What next level of automation can you apply to an existing human-based process? Can you deploy AI-infused chatbots or kiosks into a service center or registration desk? Can you build an automated process machine that speeds a process in the way that the ATM sped up dispensing cash? If your company is typical, you probably have half a dozen processes ripe for robotic process automation (RPA).

  In Chapter 7 we describe the rapid shift in which the new machine will begin to manage most, if not all, portions of certain key processes.

These will include areas such as claims processing, accounts payable and receivable, legal discovery, service desk incident resolution, network security management, and large portions of customer service and support.

In the next five years, this will be the new battleground for cost savings and performance enhancement with the new machine in that the stakes will be high and the economic incentives massive. For example, with initial implementations of RPA, we typically see more than 60% cost savings in the daily operations of a core process, with error rates plummeting to near zero. Although such results will garner many headlines, both good and bad, it will only be the beginning of the automation story.

- **Halo:** What products can you put a digital "halo" around with instrumentation, thus creating new commercial models? What "dumb" objects can become "smart?" What data can you generate that can help you "see" things that were previously invisible, such as the performance of a rotor blade in a turbine?

  In our book on Code Halos, we outlined that any noun—any person, place, or thing—had a digital self and a physical self, and we predicted that by 2020, any product costing more than $5 that you couldn't eat would be instrumented.[5] Well, Marc Andreessen has taken that further by predicting that in 20 years, *every* physical item will have a chip implanted in it.[6] Thus, as a default, you should start thinking about instrumenting all the key products and machines in your business model, and putting a halo around them all. In Chapter 8 we explain how to create commercial value from such efforts.

- **Enhance:** Which human efforts can be enhanced by the new machine, driving new levels of employee productivity and customer satisfaction? In Chapter 9, we outline how the machine becomes the new "colleague" of your front-line workers, enhancing their efforts and helping your company reach entirely new performance thresholds.

- **Abundance:** How can you leverage the new machine to drive down the price point of your products or services to be able to compete and win in low-cost, high-volume markets—markets of abundance? With the new machine, which of your products or services could be sold for 10 times less? Not 5% less, but 90% less. This may sound like madness, a prescription to destroy your revenues. However, what if it led to a new abundance, to markets that might be 100 times the size of your current market? In Chapter 10 we provide tactics for identifying your own abundance markets.

- **Discovery:** What areas of true invention are now available to you? How much of your focus and budget is devoted to initiatives that *won't* pay off this year but have enormous potential in the years ahead? If it's infinitesimal, you likely have a future relevancy issue. In 1910, as the Model T gained popularity, few could have envisioned the new markets to be discovered. Who could have predicted suburbia, the big-box retailer (e.g., Walmart), fast food (e.g., McDonald's), and national hotel chains (e.g., Holiday Inn)? Yet, these were all inventions that were derived from the initial invention of the mass-produced automobile.

    What new discoveries reside in your company? And, importantly, how can *you* leverage the new machine to revolutionize your R&D process? In Chapter 11, we outline the new process for invention.

Those that are successful in their digital initiatives tend to be very clear-headed about their goal. They balance each of these five value levers; be it the automation of a business process, boosting the value of an existing product by harnessing the data that surrounds it, enhancing human activities with digital tools, enabling mass-market consumption of your market offerings, or creating an entirely new offering with technology-based invention. They then utilize the right teams, methods, and budgets to pursue that goal. Each of these end-states requires its own path for digital reinvention, and all associated energies need to be focused on that goal. There is no such thing as a one-size-fits-all model, and firms that naïvely follow such an approach quickly encounter trouble.

The Management Opportunity of a Generation

We see many industrial-model leaders investing heavily to become hybrid winners. This book is filled with lessons of these hybrids under construction: GE, Philips, McGraw-Hill, Nike, Under Armour, Toyota. In looking at the statements of intent from their CEOs, a pattern quickly emerges:

- "It's absurd that you know more about your car than you know about your body. . . . [Under Armour Connected Fitness will] fundamentally affect global health." Kevin Plank, CEO, Under Armour[7]
- "If we are to ensure that healthcare remains affordable and widely available for future generations, we need to radically rethink how we

provide and manage it . . . and apply the technology that can help achieve these changes." Frans van Houten, CEO, Royal Philips[8]

- "Industrial companies are in the information business whether they want to be or not. . . . Now, add to that a series of decisions every company needs to make: 'Do I outsource all of that? Do I do it myself? Do I change my business model accordingly?' The decision we've made [at General Electric] is that we just want to be all in." Jeff Immelt, CEO, General Electric[9]

- "Toyota Connected will help free our customers from the tyranny of technology. It will make lives easier and help us to return to our humanity. From telematics services that learn from your habits and preferences, to use-based insurance pricing models that respond to actual driving patterns, to connected vehicle networks that can share road condition and traffic information, our goal is to deliver services that make lives easier." Zack Hicks, CEO, Toyota Connected[10]

- "You know, when I first joined the company, a long time ago, we were a manufacturing company. As we go forward, I want us to be known as a manufacturing, a technology, and an information company. Because as our vehicles become a part of the Internet of Things, and as consumers choose to share their data with us, we want to be able to use that data to help make their lives better. And also, create some business models that will help us earn a return. That's where we're heading." Mark Fields, CEO, Ford Motor Co.[11]

"Radically rethink." "Fundamentally affect." "Help us return to our humanity." "We just want to be all in." These are words spoken by CEOs who are doing the hard work to rewire their companies for the Fourth Industrial Revolution, to define and implement the new business models.

This is the management challenge of a generation. Let's now explore how to successfully take action against it.

7 | Automate

The Robots Aren't Coming; They're Here

When was the last time you went into a bank and wrote a check to get cash? Went into a travel agency to book a flight? Created a font to make a PowerPoint presentation? Can't remember? We can't either. All those things that people *used* to do have been automated away.

Now, look around you in the office where you work. See what Fred's doing? See what Anika's doing? Look at what you're doing. Lots of those things are about to be automated away too.

As we've pointed out repeatedly in the previous chapters of this book, we are riding on the cusp of a huge new wave of automated "white-collar" work that is going to fundamentally change what millions and millions of people all around the world do, Monday through Friday, 9 to 5.

For a manager, automating existing parts of your business with the new machine provides a once-in-a-generation opportunity to change the cost structure of your firm, while at the same time increasing the velocity and quality of your operations.

The automation of the processes at the core of your organization is going to make the last 25 years of Six Sigma, business process reengineering, and outsourcing seem like an overture before the main symphony begins. While each has provided many benefits (and some tears) along the way, all will pale in comparison to the impact of digitizing your core processes. In the next few pages, we cover several aspects of these automation dynamics: what automation actually is, which parts of your business are the best candidates to be automated, which jobs will be most impacted, the benefits you can expect, and the problems to avoid.

Like many things, the decisions you have to make in creating the future of your work boil down at the end of the day to simple economics. Applying new machines to your long-standing core business processes can drive not just 3% to 6% of cost out of portions of your operations but 30% to 60% (or more). If this sounds like hyperbole, recall our study that showed business already reducing costs by an average of 8% while growing revenue by an average of 10% (as shown in Figure 7.1).[1] These numbers add up, but there's more to come. Consider that companies such as TriZetto (a Cognizant health care software subsidary) are using software robots to decrease health care payer costs by as much as 90% for some middle-office business processes. Other companies such as Blue Prism are applying bots to risk, fraud, claims processing, and loan management in banking to provide similar savings.[2] (See Figure 7.2 for a range of integrated industry-specific processes that are driving significant value.)

Companies that are not taking advantage of automation are already paying a significant "laggard penalty," which will inhibit future investment.[3] Very simply, if you wish to compete at the Amazon cost and the Google speed, you have to automate significant portions of your operations during the next few years.

Automation Is Not Optional

Automation is the first step in the journey of what economist Joseph Schumpeter termed "creative destruction"—that is, the tendency for industrial change to continuously destroy old economic structures and create new ones.[4]

Respondents were asked to estimate average cost decrease (or increase) and average revenue increase (or decrease) in terms of percentage.

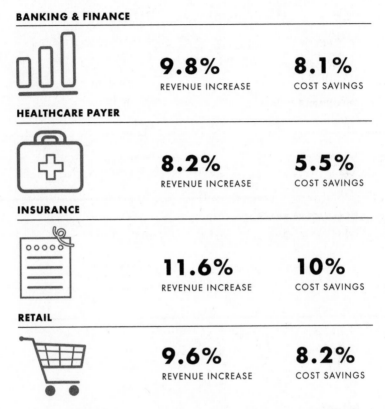

BANKING & FINANCE

9.8%
REVENUE INCREASE

8.1%
COST SAVINGS

HEALTHCARE PAYER

8.2%
REVENUE INCREASE

5.5%
COST SAVINGS

INSURANCE

11.6%
REVENUE INCREASE

10%
COST SAVINGS

RETAIL

9.6%
REVENUE INCREASE

8.2%
COST SAVINGS

Response base: 281 (respondents experiencing revenue growth due to digital process change); 200 (respondents experiencing cost reduction due to digital process change)

Source: Cognizant Center for the Future of Work.

Figure 7.1 Digital Process Change Drives Significant Top- and Bottom-Line Impact

This may sound a bit drastic, but to make it a bit clearer and less melodramatic, let's take a trip back to a newsroom during the Reagan administration.

When Paul went to journalism school in the 1980s, newsrooms were full of people who could take information from different sources and turn it into a clear, concise narrative. The daily process of news-making—collection,

Percent of respondents citing "significant" or "high" levels of process/value chain integration, as a result of digitized processes.

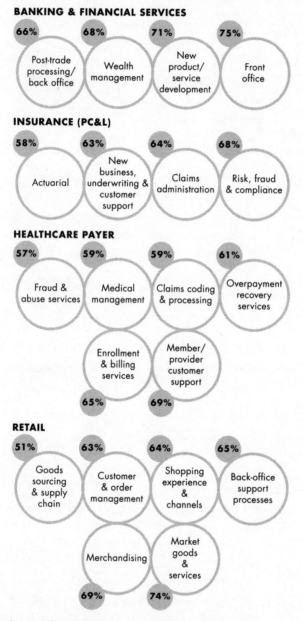

BANKING & FINANCIAL SERVICES

66% Post-trade processing/ back office
68% Wealth management
71% New product/ service development
75% Front office

INSURANCE (PC&L)

58% Actuarial
63% New business, underwriting & customer support
64% Claims administration
68% Risk, fraud & compliance

HEALTHCARE PAYER

57% Fraud & abuse services
59% Medical management
59% Claims coding & processing
61% Overpayment recovery services

Enrollment & billing services 65%
Member/ provider customer support 69%

RETAIL

51% Goods sourcing & supply chain
63% Customer & order management
64% Shopping experience & channels
65% Back-office support processes

Merchandising 69%
Market goods & services 74%

Response base: 281
Source: Cognizant Center for the Future of Work.

Figure 7.2   Putting Customers in the Center of the Value Chain, Digitally

reporting, fact–checking, synthesis, writing, and communicating—required people, lots of people, with education, judgment, and moxie. High IQ, high EQ (emotional quotient), and gallons of coffee.

Nobody in 1986 could have imagined that within 40 years, large portions of that activity would be replaced by a computer. But fast-forward to today, and that is exactly what is happening.

In the past year, you have probably read dozens of news stories written by a bot without realizing it. These have appeared in *The Washington Post*, *USA Today*, your local newspaper, and online news sources such as Yahoo! and ESPN. That real-estate listing in your neighborhood, local weather forecasts, and updates on your investment portfolio are increasingly being written not by a cub reporter but by software developed by companies like Narrative Science or Automated Insights. And this isn't isolated; it's happening at scale and continuing to grow. The Associated Press alone now publishes more than 20,000 software-written news stories a year,[5] and Automated Insights' software generated nearly 1.5 billion stories last year, personalized down to the individual level.[6]

Many of these news stories aren't just simple regurgitations of data, like the weather forecast or stock performance. Automation platforms are generating nuanced language, woven into a true narrative that is engaging, friendly, fresh, insightful . . . in fact, well, human. For example, look at the beginning of a story on a local high school baseball game in Tennessee:

Oak Ridge Wildcat Matt McDaniel Belts Two Homers That Lead to 10–8 Win over Bearden

Tuesday was a great day for Matt McDaniel, as he clubbed two home runs to carry the Wildcats to a 10–8 victory over Bearden at Farragut High School in seven innings.[7]

We could go on with more of the story, but you probably already get the point: that it was all written by a system of intelligence. The language is colloquial and aligned with both the local culture and the sport of baseball: "belts two homers," "clubbed two home runs."

Using software robot "journalists," news organizations have automated some of the basic processes of standardized reporting, including data collection, synthesis, writing, and distribution. Once the baseball game's scorecard data is loaded into the bot, the only real "action" is telling the system to produce the written output and then sending it to the required distribution channel (which, as an aside, is automated as well). During the past few years, more than 10,000 stories on minor league baseball have been produced in this way.[8]

Will news automation expand to the type of investigative reporting found on the front page of the *The New York Times* or *The Wall Street Journal*? Not likely soon (although bots will certainly enhance the capabilities of investigative journalists). But it has already had a significant impact in helping an industry—one under massive cost pressure—find great levels of efficiency while providing additional value to its customers.

This story isn't just about automating journalism. This trend—applying automation technology to lower cost and improve productivity—is playing out in nearly every industry. Like it or not, your competitor across the street will soon gain the massive benefit of digital automation of core processes. If you don't keep pace, your cost structure will soon be unsustainable. Additionally, the savings generated through automation are what will then pay for the coming digital innovations. Fortunately, most of us have a running start.

We Have Been Automating with Digital for Some Time

The way in which Narrative Science or Automated Insights is automating journalism and other writing-based activities such as stock-performance reporting is very sophisticated and represents a new frontier of robotics. However, again, let's not forget we've been consuming automation for a long time, and much as with AI, once used it's not even noticed.

Consider the last time you went to the airport. During your drive, you likely passed through an E-ZPass tollbooth on the highway. Pulling into the airport parking lot, a machine dispensed your parking pass. In the terminal, you received your ticket and checked your bags at a kiosk. Then walking to your gate, you stopped at the ATM to get cash for your trip.

Some two decades ago, people were working at each of those spots: the tollbooth attendant, the parking garage attendant, the airline clerk, and the

Figure 7.3   Familiar Automation in Our Daily Lives

bank teller. Yet, many (but not all) of those jobs have been automated away (others have been enhanced with technology, which we'll cover later), and as a consumer you are probably grateful.

From your house to the airport gate, your trip was at least a half-hour faster than in pre-automation days. And is anybody really nostalgic about the tollbooth attendant, that poor soul who had to stand in that cold metal box for eight hours, making change, breathing in exhaust, all the while creating long lines for the rest of us? Not even the ex-tollbooth attendant wants that job to come back.

With the new machine, we are now crossing a line to making "intelligent" processes truly intelligent. The new waves of automation are popping up all around us, yet unlike the EZPass scanners over the highway, they are both so subtle and powerful (as in robo-journalism) that they may even go unnoticed.

Software Should Be Eating Your Core Operations

In your company, exactly where will such automation take place? The best areas are in your core operations, tucked away from customers. Automation's low-hanging fruit—massive cost savings found in the guts of your operations—is in what we refer to as your back and middle offices.

Your back office includes core functions that support any corporation: information technology, finance, human resources, facilities management, administration, and so on. The middle office encompasses the industry-specific core processes that run across your value chain: claims processing in insurance, logistics management in retail, trade settlement in banking.

What if you could run these functions or processes at half the cost and with double the throughput? With continuous improvement and quality control? And with all aspects—every transaction—fully instrumented and recorded? With the new machine, you can.

As with journalism, these areas of your business, at their core, comprise an information supply chain that gathers, synthesizes, transforms, and distributes data. The list of candidates, as shown in Figure 7.4, is so extensive as to be surprising.

Each and every one of these areas has an intelligent automation solution focused on it and available for deployment: AiCure for clinical data science; Talla for HR management; NextAngles for compliance reporting in financial services. Kevin Kelly, founder of *Wired* magazine, has gone as far as to say the business plans of the next 10,000 Silicon Valley start-ups are easy to forecast: "Take X and add AI."[9]

While the following lists may be useful, given that these are all areas in which the new machine is being implemented for automation purposes, how do you find *your* best candidates? After all, the same process from one company to another may be structured very differently. One man's ceiling is another man's floor.

BACK OFFICE AUTOMATION CANDIDATES

Finance & Accounting:
- Accounts payable
- Accounts receivable
- Order to cash
- Invoice auditing/processing
- Compliance control and regulation
- Order management
- Trade quote automation
- Procurement/sourcing
- Records to report (RTR)
- Billing management

Human Resources:
- Automated payroll processing
- Tax changes, benefits enrollment, open enrollment
- Employee data management
- Claims management
- Application tracking
- Onboarding/Off-boarding
- Query management

Information Technology:
- Cybersecurity/fraud detection
- Infrastructure services: server maintenance, version upgrades
- Cloud-based solutions using IPA implementation
- Network systems, external interfaces
- Legacy systems consolidation
- Software asset management (SAM)

Customer Service:
- Query management
- Billing support
- Complaint management
- Order processing
- Subscription management
- Help desk management
- Sales support

Figure 7.4   Potential Process Automation Opportunities

MIDDLE OFFICE AUTOMATION CANDIDATES

Insurance:

- Fraud detection
- Critical "checks and measures" for data authenticity
- Policy service and contract administration
- Agent onboarding
- Claims administration, including recognition and classification of claims
- Risk, fraud, and compliance
- Enhancement of supplier collaboration in bulk payments and recoveries typically involved in insurance claims
- Contact center automation

Health Care:

- Enrollment and billing
- Accelerate claims processing, mass uploads, and reconciliations
- EHR/EMR audit of all data
- Simplified access to patient data in legacy systems
- Embedment of RPA in labor-intensive, error prone processes (accelerated workflows)
- Claims administration (claims process optimization)
- Enrollment and eligibility
- Billing and payments
- Patient scheduling
- Records management

Banking/Capital Markets:

- Credit card administration
- Automating credit card fraud management (including account closures and chargeback processes)
- Asset management
- Consumer loans and lending
- Trade settlement
- Enhanced customer query resolution timeframes
- Enhancement of accuracy and compliancy levels
- Contact center automation
- Automating the redemption of funds from stocks and shares

Life Sciences:

- Clinical data science
- Complaint management
- Regulatory tracking
- Customer interaction
- Procure to pay
- Invoice processing
- Quote to cash
- Customer setup
- Serious adverse event reconciliation
- Adverse event comparison
- Narrative writing

Technology:

- Contract management
- E-discovery/digital asset management
- Revenue/liabilities management
- Process automation/augmentation (HR/legal/finance)
- Initiative tracking/reporting (BI)
- Entitlements tracking/management/SLAs
- Onboarding/off-boarding/resource tracking
- Billing and order management
- Procurement/supply chain
- Quote to cash (Q2C)

Consumer Packaged Goods (CPG):

- Automating manual processes in data extraction and validation processes
- Order management
- Reporting
- Automating data transformation of multiple input files received from multiple systems (e.g., ERP)
- Contact center automation

Figure 7.4   Potential Process Automation Opportunities (*continued*)

TriZetto Automates the U.S. Health Care Business

The U.S. health care industry, worth $3 trillion in 2014, is one of the largest and most complex industries in the world.[10] It's also one of the most ripe for automation-based reform. According to some estimates, one-third of all spending on U.S. health care is completely wasted.[11]

Colorado-based TriZetto was founded 20 years ago with a mission to bring the power of automation to bear on this dysfunctional system. As one of the first software-as-a-service vendors, TriZetto pioneered the ideas of applying multi-tenancy and platforms to the management of the processes that run some of the market's biggest health care payers (the insurance companies) and providers (the hospitals and health care groups). As of 2015, TriZetto processed 60% of U.S. health care claims, and in the same year it was acquired by Cognizant for $2.7 billion.

Early in its journey, TriZetto leadership realized that the real value of the company's offering was in using software to automate high-volume, routinized work in the payer space (e.g., the many steps that happen behind the scenes of your health insurance provider in the United States). Given that health care regulations in the United States require at least 85% of costs to be related to health care, and no more than 15% of costs to administration, to be competitive, providers must lower their costs as much as possible while keeping care quality constant. To help make this happen, over the years TriZetto has built and bought various software assets to automate and improve many health care insurance back-office work processes, such as care planning, care management, payments, and so on.

We spoke with Lawrence Bridge, senior vice president of strategy and corporate development, who explained that automation not only reduces cost but also helps provide better health care outcomes. "Tools that we're bringing to market, such as Healthcare Productivity Automation (HPA), are able to essentially eliminate a lot of the manual processes," he said.

The operational results are, in a word, stunning. The "before" picture of how a claim is processed, according to Bridge, involves 120 people sitting in cubicles working with a lot of paper and largely outdated IT systems. In the "after" picture, implemented within a matter of weeks, one person works with a system of intelligence to process the same volume of claims. "Now the team is working to expand their automation capability to customer service and other work that has traditionally required a human worker, including, eventually, actual medical care," Bridge said.

In TriZetto's work, automation does not equal immediate job loss. While some jobs are certainly eliminated, many others are redeployed in response to growing demand for a wide range of other services. Health care in the United States is moving from a centralized model to a more consumer-focused one. An increasing number of insured people—due to the Affordable Care Act—along with growing health care needs due to an aging population, is resulting in an overall increase in demand for health care. This demand requires both people and machines to succeed. "You could never do this without automation. It would take a million people," Bridge said. "But now, you've got government regulations compressing and shaping the cost and spend curves. You've got technology maturing at a crazy rate. . . . So it's the perfect storm to drive . . . this mass personalization model in the health care payer space."

Even if you're not in the health care payer business, you can take away some key automation lessons from TriZetto for your company:

- **Focus on a high-volume core business process.** TriZetto applies software to routinized recurring work in the middle office of health care payers. There is literally no company we've worked with that could not apply this same approach. Every company has automation possibilities. Our job now is to figure out where we can apply new systems of intelligence to routinized, high-volume, and often mind-numbing business processes. (More on this follows.)
- **Be bold.** TriZetto leaders build tools to automate work, so they know what's realistic vs. theoretical. Their rule of thumb is to shoot for 50% automation of an existing process. Targeting 4% or 5% is simply not enough to make it worthwhile. If you start out willing to accept less than 25% automation, you are undoubtedly aiming too low.
- **Find the patterns.** Automation is a scale play. Companies deploying automation well achieve the most gains by eliminating custom solutions. As Bridge put it, "The companies that . . . really well defined their benefit programs or very much defined their provider

contracts. . . . were the ones able to auto-adjudicate and drive standardization. . . . The ones that really won historically were the ones able to get standardization, replicability, and consistent procedure. When we look forward, I think it's going to be all about the use of digital, both on the administrative and the health care cost side of the business."

What to Do on Monday? Flick Your Automation-On Switch

Automation doesn't happen automatically. To that end, here are some lessons learned from those who have implemented process automation to help kick-start your automation initiatives. We have found these four "rules of the road" to be particularly useful:

1. Set your 25%–25% automation imperative.
2. Find your process-automation targets.
3. Break through the "brass wall."
4. Build a repeatable process to obliterate work.

Set Your 25%–25% Automation Imperative

When you walk into work, (nearly) everyone has a purpose. Things hum along pretty much the same way, every day. On any given Monday morning, it's almost impossible to imagine work being done differently. But this is exactly what you need to do first. To begin any meaningful change using automation, you must suspend disbelief and imagine that things can be done in an entirely new way.

We think your baseline expectation should be cost reductions of 25%, with an associated productivity increase of 25%. Based on where the current average is today (around 15%), and the productivity improvement seen by some solutions (up to 90%), this should be your achievable near-term rule of thumb for initial robotic process automation efforts.

The reason the 25%–25% rule is effective is that it forces your team to think differently about "the way things are done around here." When the goals are, say, 5% cost savings or 5% productivity gains, your team will continue to think in traditional ways. By raising the bar to 25%–25%, it will quickly become clear that the traditional cocktail of reorganization, outsourcing, and/or enterprise software will not be good enough. Only the digital automation of the process will deliver such results. Put simply, if you cannot gain at least 25% cost savings, you don't have a real "automation" solution. And if you cannot find 25% productivity increases, then the AI platform is not performing as it should.

In addition, you need to create a "no-excuses" environment. There will be those who push back, saying—for various reasons—"that can't be done." Yet it's becoming clear there are no true hurdles with technology, cost, or scale. Once you set that goal, it's time to pick your spots.

Find Your Process-Automation Targets

When looking for your initial automation opportunities, which should be no more than two or three processes, you should "pick your spots" on the human-machine work continuum (see Figure 7.5). The best automation starting points are to the left of the continuum; in these processes, the machine can rapidly take over the majority of the work effort. As we described in Chapter 3, these should be areas with a high percentage of work tasks that can be automated.

You need to be thoughtful when selecting your first automation targets, because the success, or lack thereof, of these initial implementations will dictate your subsequent enterprise AI initiatives. In our work with dozens of intelligent automation initiatives, we've seen that the successful ones all meet these simple criteria:

- **Highly repetitive tasks:** Find tasks that are highly repetitive but that occur at great scale within your organization. In short, look for activities

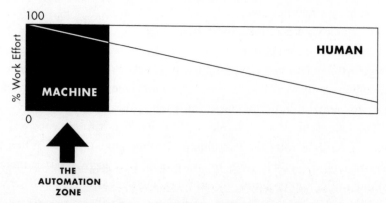

Figure 7.5   The Human–Machine Work Continuum

that lots of people do every day. It could be processing an invoice, proofreading documentation, "picking and packing," reconciling orders, answering the same questions over and over on the phone, and so on. Many of these tasks are already heavily automated; but many, in our observation, are not. Give yourself an honest answer: Are these areas—and many more—as fully automated as they could be? And is there intelligence in the current process? Any high-volume, highly repetitive task is a prime candidate for automation.

- **Tasks with low demand for human judgment:** Robots are great at calculation; humans less so. Conversely, humans are better at complex judgments, while AI and algorithms are not. Thus, jobs that lean heavily on decision trees (as opposed to ambiguity, intuition, insight, complex judgment) are strong candidates for automation. Machines may be able to inform decisions, but making more nuanced judgment calls will for the foreseeable future require a human touch. Conversely, any job that's mostly a series of "if-this-then-that" steps should be automated.

- **Tasks requiring low levels of empathy:** Order entry, claims adjudication, and invoice reconciliation are processes that require accuracy, consistency, and speed . . . but rarely empathy. If a bot can materially boost accuracy, consistency, and speed, many of us will settle for dumping the empathy factor. There are many areas within your organization right now to which that logic can be applied. It won't be hard to find them.

- **Tasks generating and handling high volumes of data:** Any process with the potential for generating lots of data, particularly customer data, should be automated for the sole purpose of collecting that data—your proprietary raw material. Humans, even if you can afford enough of them, will not be able to deal with the volumes of data when more and more "things" become smart and connected. As one simple example, imagine when all the street lights in a medium-size city are "smart" and able to report on not only their own "health" (i.e., whether they need replacing) but can also report on vehicle traffic flows. The volumes of data generated by this type of city-wide information "mesh" will be far beyond the human capacity to manage and make sense of it. In scenarios like this, automation won't replace people but will be a fundamental building block of creating new services and new insights that in turn will generate new value. In your organization, you should look for areas in which processes and workflows can be sensor-enabled and from which transaction data, previously unavailable, can be generated and managed.

Identifying your automation targets will give your teams a clear path to success, but there still remains a significant hurdle in managing change within your organization. That leads to our third rule of the road.

Break Through the "Brass Wall"

OK, you may have identified your initial automation targets, which are being pursued across your industry and clearly pass the 25%–25% threshold. Everyone in your company will see the wisdom of your decision and will be fully supportive, right? Wrong.

We learned this lesson 20 years ago during the aforementioned business process reengineering (BPR) wave. Back in the 1990s, acolytes of Michael Hammer proclaimed, "Don't automate. Obliterate!" The mantra was to find ways to deliver more with less—way less.

BPR, in theory, was very sound. Yet, in most cases, the practice failed (widely soiling the name of the movement in the process). Why? Quite often, the very middle managers who were responsible for architecting and implementing BPR initiatives soon figured out they were reengineering themselves out of a job. Politics and sabotage ensued.

In hindsight, this was the "brass wall" phenomenon, which was first seen with reengineering efforts within police forces of major cities in the United States during the 1980s. During the explosion of drug-trade-related violence, police chiefs in New York, Boston, Miami, and Los Angeles all looked to establish new ways of policing (e.g., more cops walking the beat, following the "broken windows" philosophy of addressing even the smallest of crimes, leveraging data for smarter policing, and flattening the organization model to remove bureaucracy and cost). The people at the top of the policing pyramid (e.g., the police chief and his or her team, as well as municipal leaders) were hugely supportive, looking to drive the change. Young police officers, living with the frustration of the existing system, were largely supportive of these new policing techniques, as well. Yet, such change efforts were initially halted by the "brass wall"—the officers sitting in the middle of the pyramid (those with brass on their shoulders), who were at least a couple of decades into their careers, had earned their way into seniority and the power structure, and could begin to smell their pensions. To them, the perceived personal threat of such changes greatly outweighed any potential community benefits.

This brass-wall phenomenon is reappearing in today's corporate environment with digital automation initiatives. Senior employees may recognize, "Yes, automation is good for our customers and investors, but is it good for me?" Rarely are their comments so direct. Instead, you will be hit with issues, such as "That's impossible." "It's too expensive." "We'll get in trouble with regulators." "We've done it this way for 50 years, and it's working fine." "Nobody can prove the ROI today." "We should focus our efforts elsewhere."

This is a tough problem to solve, but solve it you must. We recommend identifying the most vocal proponents of "business as usual," talking to them, and explaining to them the reality of what automation means for the organization. Invite them to "get with the program" and help their colleagues get with it too. If they can't, avoid them and have them focus their energies elsewhere. And if there are no other opportunities available in other parts of your organization, let them go (of course following all the proper HR protocols). Achieving the goals of automation is too important to allow failure to happen due to the intransigence of employees whose skills and experience are no longer a good fit for work infused with systems of intelligence.

As we stated earlier, there will be blood; automation will hurt. Nobody said this would be easy. But automation is a fact of life, and facts of life need to be faced.

Build a Repeatable Process to Obliterate Work

Once you've set bold goals for making automation happen and have chosen solid targets that will lead to business impact, the next step is to convert work from "Then Margaret in procurement does this" to "Beep. Done." This is how you go about doing that.

In every case of successful automation we've seen, a creative business leader looked at how a process was being executed; concluded "We really stink at this"; and found a better way of using code, artificial intelligence, and algorithms to improve the speed, accuracy, and cost profile of the process.

Additionally, these leaders realized they need to apply the new tools, which may be fairly simple or incredibly sophisticated, to automate very specific process steps. Regardless of whether you are re-creating a business process from scratch or injecting a tried-and-true automation technology into middle- or back-office processes, there is a path you should follow.

You will need to adapt the path depending on the complexity of what you're doing; what follows is a high-level walkthrough, but the seven steps for automating any process or task are basically the same:

1. **Set your automation strategy**. As discussed previously, the first step is setting a bold vision for applying the new machines to reduce costs. You simply can't skip this one.

2. **Start small.** In spite of the large potential benefits of automation, it's a best practice to start small. Begin by finding a few pressure points in key processes. General proclamations of "do automation" are a waste of time. Every successful automation example we've seen has been focused on a specific task or business process. What is a "process pressure point?" Typically, it's a bottleneck that frustrates everybody today (e.g., payments, mortgage loan applications, medical records management, travel planning, etc.).

3. **Apply the new machines**. This is where "market sensing" will pay off. (We have more on this in Chapter 10 on abundance.) Identify the relevant automation tools that already exist and test them out in a limited trial. Of course, if there are no commercially available tools for the process you are looking to automate, you may need to build your own AI platform.[12] This will certainly be more complicated; look to buy before you build.

4. **Develop a prototype**. You have a strategy, some process targets, and a few potential automation machines. It's time now to put the pieces together, but you need to start with a prototype. This phase includes blueprinting and the first rough build of your automation engine applied to your specific context. You'll need the data, the machine, and a clear understanding of what happens before, during, and after the automation activity. When an automation tool already exists, this may require only minor configuration. If, on the other hand, you're building a new engine, this can take some time. The output of this step is a prototype that more or less works in a controlled environment. There will be bugs, and there'll be plenty of people saying it doesn't work, but you need to exit this step with enough of a working system to warrant moving to a production environment.

5. **Pilot and scale**. Now it's time for real work to be affected. As with any big change, discretion is the better part of valor, so start small—for example, a subset of the work, a single store, some customer interactions. All the questions around security, privacy, and compliance must be resolved, and people's experiences should be assessed to avoid heading into a knowledge-process industrial accident.

6. **Analyze the results**. What has the pilot told you? What have you learned? What went well? What didn't go so well? Be honest; be critical. Look for reasons to say, "No, this isn't working." Pivot; adjust; recalibrate. Stay resolute.

7. **Repeat!** The requirement to automate is a constant, so no single project will ensure success in the digital economy.

These seven steps should be the foundation for reaching the next level of automation in your organization.[13]

Automation Is a Means, Not an End

This chapter has focused on the practical aspects of automation in the corporation: where it is occurring today, how to pick your spots, the critical success factors, and what you should expect on the journey. We've shown that robotic process automation is our new loom, our new steam engine. The cost savings generated from these next levels of automation will provide the cash needed to fuel investment in new markets and new ideas. The data generated by automation is at the heart of creating new products, better customer relationships, and more transparency. Leaders who create the ongoing momentum for using automation—every quarter looking for new automation opportunities using the criteria and guidelines we've presented—will ensure they have the fuel needed to win.

If you're managing work that is ripe for automation, it's not a time for talk, to simply say, "We are on the cusp of change!" It's time to get busy. If your company's rooms are full of people doing work that can be automated, it's time to realize that is not sustainable.

And finally, you need to realize and remember that the future of work doesn't stop at "A," automation. There are four more value levers in our model to go: "H," "E," "A," and "D." Automation is not an end in its own right, it is simply a means to an end. In the next chapter, we'll look at "H"— how you can build halos of meaningful data, make everything a "code generator," and convert that data into dollars (and pounds, and euros, and yen).

8 | Halo

Instrument Everything, Change the Game

Several years ago, we wrote *Code Halos* to outline how any "noun"—any person, place, or thing—actually has both a physical self and a virtual self. Once instrumented and tracked, an invisible halo of code emerges around the object, and this "digital twin" often provides more insight and value than the actual physical item itself.

This is how, having never met you as a consumer in person, Amazon and Netflix know your tastes in literature and movies better than your family and friends do. These halos are central to how the FANG vendors can build such personal and valuable customer relationships.

In the time since we wrote that book, winning with data has since gone mainstream, and leveraging Code Halos has become a strategic imperative for nearly every type of business. The race is on to win through instrumentation, and established companies are changing the rules of competition across many industries, including:

- **Industrial machinery:** Bosch, John Deere, Caterpillar, General Electric, Siemens, Boeing, and Airbus, with combined revenues approaching

$500 billion annually, view halo-based competition as central to their strategies, as they are all now instrumenting their machines as a default. Whereas these firms until recently competed on only physical aspects—the quality, price/performance, and safety of their products—they are now focused on the value of the virtual.

- **Athletic apparel:** Nike, Adidas, and Under Armour are all looking at annual growth rates of more than 15% between 2015 and 2020—with Under Armour aiming to double in size during that time—based on the power of instrumented shoes and clothing.[1] In the process, these companies are transitioning from new-age cobblers to health information platforms.
- **Automobiles:** Toyota, BMW, Ford, GM, Mercedes-Benz, and Tesla are investing a combined $6 billion in digitization capabilities, primarily focusing on revolutionizing the automobile through instrumentation. Doing so will redefine not just the car but also car ownership and driving itself.
- **Insurance:** Progressive, Allstate, and Travelers are leading the charge in telematics devices, as the instrumentation of cars, homes, and buildings promises to transform customer relationships along with actuarial science itself through real-time asset monitoring. The traditional insurance model, based on static and one-to-many customer engagements, is soon to become context based, situational, and one-to-one.

There is now no limitation, technical or financial, for connecting anything to the Internet and then infusing it with the brilliance of a system of intelligence.

The question now is: What to do about it.

Every "Thing" Is Now a Code Generator

The cost of instrumenting everything is now too low, and the potential value too high, to avoid. As we noted in *Code Halos*:

> [Winners in the digital economy] have mastered the ability to create and manage the Code Halos surrounding their customers, products, services, and entire organizations to establish new thresholds of performance. In wrapping those widgets with digits, they have created highly personalized customer experiences, products, and services that deliver not just utility but also insight and meaning at unassailable levels of efficiency.[2]

Boeing's Digital Airline, Philips's connected lighting systems, and Toyota's smart cars are all examples of these ideas being applied in the enterprise context. In each case, business leaders are turning their key products into code generators, thus creating the raw materials (data) for the digital economy. Algorithms and AI, integrated into systems of intelligence, convert that data into valuable insights that drive business outcomes.

With all this activity, the failure to take action at this point and turn "things" into code generators could almost be considered corporate malpractice. To get started, here are some key tactics to making this work in your world.

Three New Rules of Competition

After helping hundreds of clients learn how to compete on code over the past few years, we have identified three key principles for success:

- **Instrumentation is no longer elective; it is now core curriculum.** Code Halos *began* in the media and entertainment markets, but they don't *end* there. As recently as 2013, many thought the digital movement would be isolated to a handful of industries and would not expand into nearly every industry you can name, as it has done.
- **Code is more valuable than things.** The value of code can often meet or exceed the value of any physical device. Many view this as "turning water into wine," as traditional products are transformed into platforms that seal customer relationships. A running shoe of old is the data platform of today, and the virtual has as much or even more value than the physical.
- **Never turn them off.** Instrumenting every "thing" also means making it continually connected to the Internet. Value can't grow exponentially when engagement is an episodic, once-in-a-while thing. Connections with data need to be always-on.

For a specific example of how these three principles are playing out in the market, let's take a look at a health insurer in Johannesburg, South Africa.

Step Away from the Donut!

Founded in 1992, Discovery Limited provides integrated financial services, including life and health insurance, to more than 6.9 million people (primarily in South Africa but also in the UK, Europe, the United States, China, Asia, and Australia). The company has successfully integrated the new raw materials, new machines, and new business models to modernize a very traditional—some might say stodgy—business.

Brett Tromp, chief financial officer, and Emile Stipp, chief actuary, explained that government regulation in South Africa required that everyone have access to health insurance and that everyone must pay the same premium for coverage. As Tromp told us, "In other words, we couldn't charge a higher premium for somebody that's on their deathbed rather than somebody who is perfectly healthy. And . . . we have to accept anybody who wants to take out insurance from us. . . . We can't deny access to anybody."

This sounds like a disastrous context for an insurance business, but Discovery leaders figured out that the way to win was actually to *keep people healthy*, and they decided to use technology, coupled with a sophisticated benefit system for members, to lower health risks while building a successful business.

According to Tromp, "We couldn't just be an insurance company. We had to be an insurance company *and* a wellness company." Discovery leaders knew that the fuel for their business had to be, no surprise here, data. They needed to know things like: How many times am I going to the gym? When do I go for a run? Am I eating healthy food? What's my blood pressure, cholesterol, and BMI?

They built a system of apps and supporting systems so members can track and share this data, linking to fitness devices, food diaries, and even driving habits. It's not a one-way street though. Discovery realized that people need to "get" something meaningful in return for "giving" over their very personal data. Insurance customers who engage in healthy behavior get real benefits, including things like discounts on healthy food, reduced airfares, Apple Watches you can earn by exercising, movie tickets, and so on.

Discovery has built a thriving business based on connecting insurance customer Code Halos with benefits. If this all still sounds a bit too fuzzy and irrationally exuberant, consider that Discovery Limited's stock price nearly doubled between November 2013 and November 2015. New business was up 51% from 2014 to 2015. Discovery Health now has a 38% market share with improving profits, better savings on insurance fraud, and decreasing costs (recently down by 14%).

The Discovery Health story shows how applying Code Halo thinking can help a traditionally conservative business create new markets in a world where systems of intelligence can easily do things that were impossible only a few years ago. There are many lessons to be learned, but here are a few of the most important ones:

- **Connect the Three M's.** Discovery Health recognized that it needed to know more about healthy behaviors than ever before, so it built systems to collect that information and keep it secure. The company uses systems of intelligence, including more than 250 people employed simply to explore its massive data sets to unearth patterns (because machines still can't ask smart questions). One of its most important innovations is, of course, an entirely new business model that builds relationships around healthy behaviors for customers while driving revenue up and costs down. New raw materials, new machines, and new business models are all successfully deployed in what is traditionally considered an industry highly resistant to change.
- **Make a promise.** Many of the innovators we interviewed, when discussing how they are building new digital solutions, emphasized a focus on something beyond pure business results. Discovery's leaders said the same thing. Their focus, the promise of their business, is to make people healthy. They know if they do that, they can build a wildly successful insurance business. And that's exactly the right perspective we should all have going into the Fourth Industrial Revolution. Stipp said, "So this whole process of making people healthier [is] a central part of what we do. . . . Everything that we do stems from it. So when we see that Apple is launching a new watch [with fitness capabilities], what we thought is, 'How can we use this to make people healthier?' And our next thought is, 'If people are excited about Apple Watches and they want them, how can we use that excitement to achieve this vision?'" Every day, Discovery focuses on keeping that promise, and the results follow.

- **Build a relationship.** We focus a lot on technology in this book because it's a critical element of winning in the digital economy. Discovery's leaders know that the tools are powerful means to an end. Their ultimate goal is to use technology in a way that keeps people healthy, not to build some tremendously intrusive surveillance system because they know people would reject that. Their goal is to build an ongoing relationship with customers. "[If] you think about insurance, particularly in life insurance . . . you get your policy, sign the paper for it, and then forget about it. And then when you die, your wife thinks about the fact that you have insurance. But there's no interaction. And this changes it completely," Tromp told us. "We talk to you every day. You talk to us every day. It changes your relationship that almost no other insurance company would have."

Others we spoke with had a similar perspective. They focused first on making people healthy, supporting education, or helping with financial security, *then* they figured out how to use data, new machines, and new business models to make it happen. Success follows.

Become a "Know-It-All"

Why instrument everything and build solutions around information? Because doing so sets you on the path to being a "Know-It-All" business. With sensors and instrumentation, it's now possible to collect and analyze information about everything, to know *everything* about *everything*.

Before the advent of the Know-It-All business, the answers to many questions (e.g., real-time equipment status of an in-flight plane, the immediate impact of an economic event, a student's real-time performance on a particular assignment) were often simply guesses and would take time to figure out.

Earlier we introduced a few examples of this. To determine how a particular plane engine is performing in-flight, for example, the maintenance crew at Heathrow would collect *some* post-flight information and *sort of* have an idea of the metrics of the flight, but much of their perspective would be based on hunches and educated guesses, and would be available eight hours after the flight had landed.

To determine how an interest rate change in New Zealand would impact state-issued bonds in California, the traders at your local broker would check their Excel spreadsheets with complex equations showing the relationship between x and y, or a and b. But ask about the impact of x on b and ask them for it *now*, and the phone line would probably go quiet.

When asked how Johnny did on today's lesson in differential calculus, a teacher in a traditional school would probably have some sense of how the student was performing on a semester-to-semester basis, but he or she wouldn't know for sure whether Johnny really understood the difference between his local maxima or minima *at this very moment*.

Let's look at how General Electric (GE), one of the most venerable industrial brands in the world, is adopting this model to get more from its machines.

GE's Rolling Data Center

General Electric may be one and a quarter centuries old, but it now views itself as a software start-up. Halo thinking—and action—is now pervasive across all divisions of the company, as GE instruments its jet engines, CT scanners, power turbines, oil rigs, and locomotives to redefine customer relationships with a "digital twin" of these machines. GE is leading the Industrial Internet and pursuing the $225 billion market opportunity.[3]

By building a Code Halo around its train engines, GE can use sensor technology and analytics to provide seemingly small improvements that together lead to business gains worth billions. The company's latest locomotive, the Tier 4, is armed with over 200 sensors, and this "rolling data center" is transforming customer relationships in several ways.

- **Zero unscheduled downtime:** An instrumented machine can provide information on its own needs for predictive maintenance. Through continual collection and analysis of sensor-generated data, a machine can essentially "wave its hand," telling maintenance engineers, "I have a small problem over here that may soon turn into a large one," be it a failing valve, a clogged fuel line, or an overheating rotor. Through such instrumented and automated maintenance, GE can ensure that small problems never become large problems and that a GE machine that is often central to a customer's operations will never let them down.

- **Finding the 1%:** We all know there's waste in our daily operations. With its intelligent machines, GE can turn to its customer base and say, "Together, let's go find the low-hanging fruit. Let's find the first 1%." Spread across an entire rail network, such as that of BNSF Railway, this 1% can quickly turn into tens of millions of dollars in cost savings that drop almost instantly to the bottom line.

- **Coaching the user:** One way to find that 1% is to guide users in making the most effective decisions. In the case of GE Transportation, this could be the smart locomotive telling the engineer how to best cross a particular mountain pass. That is, the machine can advise on how to optimize fuel efficiency on the way up the mountain, and how to best utilize the brakes on the way down. This is done not in some generic fashion but mile by mile, turn by turn, based on the history of the track, the current weather, the driving style of the specific engineer, and the load being transported. The result is fuel savings of 3% to 17%.

- **No machine is an island:** A single intelligent GE Tier 4 can provide all these benefits, but a fleet of intelligent locomotives, all connected together, can take performance to another level (as shown in Figure 8.1). After all, a train is only as efficient as its network; through fleet instrumentation, GE Transportation's customers can boost the efficiency of their yard operations and rail networks by 10%.[4]

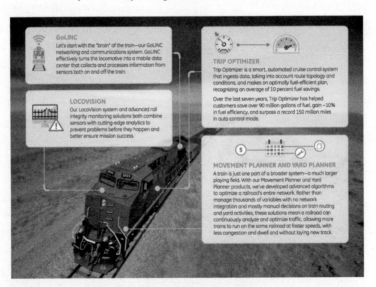

Figure 8.1   GE's Intelligent Locomotive
Source: GE Transportation

Through such efforts, it's clear how GE's (still young) Industrial Internet initiatives are changing the basis of competition in each of its industries. It's a great showcase for how every physical thing can—and should—be nearly painted with different sensors to become essential elements of systems of intelligence.

In fact, GE's moves to instrument and sensor-enable its entire portfolio of products and machines is at the core of its Industrial Internet strategy, which is at the core of its overall corporate strategy, *period*. It's no wonder why, in GE's view, the Industrial Internet is set to generate a market worth trillions of dollars by 2030. GE's CEO, Jeff Immelt, put it this way when talking about the locomotive example: "Trillions of dollars of wealth have been created in Industrial Internet stocks over the last 15 years. If you look out 10 or 15 years, there's going to be trillions of dollars of wealth created in the Industrial Internet, and we're just in the first inning."[5]

Know Your Back Office Too!

In a Know-It-All business everything can be known, *should* be known, and *must* be known. The new rules of business are based on knowing and knowing more than your competitors do. Get this right: know and win. Get this wrong: guess and lose.

As of now, using data and devices to upgrade consumer experiences is nothing new. The big work ahead is applying the same philosophy to other vital, but maybe less high-profile, aspects of enterprise work. This Know-It-All mindset is already springing to life in some common enterprise back-office processes:

- **Human resource management:** Google leverages instrumentation internally to optimize its people management by analyzing the formal, informal, and personal information its employees generate throughout the day. Google tries to know all of its roughly 57,000 employees in much more detail than is typical in a large enterprise and works to personalize career trajectories for its entire staff. Laszlo Bock, senior advisor at Google and former senior vice president of people operations (or human resources) at the company, points to the positive economic impact this approach generates: better recruitment, retention, and job satisfaction rates (all with an associated financial implication) than found at competitors. The Code Halos around its people allow Google to apply the same type of rigor to its people-based decisions as it does to its engineering decisions. Microsoft's $26 billion acquisition of LinkedIn in June 2016 is premised on a similar idea—of harvesting the data around people to inject the same type of collaboration and "social selling" that is common online into how big businesses run these types of processes.

- **Supply chain management:** The concept of building Code Halos around "things" is finding its way into global supply chains, helping manufacturers and retailers answer a growing number of questions from customers about the provenance of the goods and services they buy, such as "Where was this shirt made, and are the people who made it being treated fairly?" The shoe manufacturer Toms, as an example, uses a software product called Sourcemap to create transparency within its products' journeys from factories around the world to stores in the United States and Europe. Customers can access information on factory conditions where the shoe was made and can track the progress of the shoes they buy through sensor enablement within the end-to-end supply chain, including raw materials, manufacturing equipment, and shipping containers.

- **Smart automobiles and fleet management:** Automobiles are fast becoming the next computing platform; according to industry estimates, the average car already has 100 sensors on board and projections suggest this number will double by 2020. As such, every car is a rolling generator, sharing data that allows manufacturers, insurers, and others to know about the health and performance of each and every individual car in highly personalized detail. Offerings such as Hum from Verizon—priced at $10 per month—are attempting to put the "mass" into this "mass personal-ization." A car owner using the service can know *in real time* about the health of the car's engine, upcoming road conditions (*what exactly is the next best action?*), precisely where he or she parked (or where the car is if it's been stolen), as well as a whole range of other information. Soon, we predict this type of plug-in device will be embedded in every new car (even those that retail at budget prices). The technology is also finding its way into fleets of company cars and trucks, providing organizations with far more granular insight into shipping route performance, trip optimization, and overall fleet maintenance, than has ever been available before.

What to Do on Monday? Capitalize on Code

The case studies we've presented share a basic element: people just got started. Instead of spending months outlining grand strategies in attempts to determine every possible end state, competitor move, and customer value proposition, and then outlining detailed plans for getting there, instrumentation winners simply started by putting a chip in a machine and seeing what happened. With this as a guiding philosophy, here are some tactics you should adopt and adapt to your business.

Buy an Extra-Large Box of Chips

We've shown that getting your new raw material is the first step to building effective systems of intelligence. So, first things first; start by ordering chips with everything (well, sensors, actually). There are many types of sensor and instrumentation devices, such as RFID sensors, accelerometers, proximity sensors, motion sensors, and so on. These small, often inexpensive devices can be placed on any physical thing and can generate data (i.e., about what that thing is, its physical location, etc.) and then transmit data to a reader. RFID chips, for example, are already widely used to track goods within supply chains, manage inventory management, and verify personal information in a range of applications, such as passports, access management, and contactless payment. You may even have found one opening this book!

Soon, sensors will be embedded within most if not all physical things in the world, and even within people. In fact, over 10,000 people have chips implanted under their skin already (and millions more use medical devices that are sensor-enabled).[6] Seemingly the stuff of Hollywood and/or nightmares, human chip implants are a frontier of science that is still in its infancy but may in time seem commonplace.

Regardless of the specific sensor type (or the creepiness factor of people getting chipped like a pampered pet), the point is that instrumentation is an important building block of introducing AI and the new machines into your organization.

Simply saying "buy chips" is a bit hyperbolic, but we're making an important point: You and your team should view sensors as essentially free and ubiquitous, and apply them liberally.

Find a Squad of Data Scientists

Once your instrumentation initiatives are in flight, you will soon notice how much data is being generated. Of course, as we examined in Chapter 5, this raw data—this *raw material*—is useless unless you can do something with it. This is where data scientists come into the picture. Called, perhaps a bit wishfully, the "sexiest job of the 21st century," the data scientist's role is to find business meaning in all the data that instrumentation creates.[7]

In our recent research, however, big data and analytics were named the number-one hard-to-find competency, not just now but also for the next three years.[8] While many respondents plan to form cross-functional teams (60%) or recruit staff (58%) to fill the gap, many others (56%) plan to increase their use of contractors and sourcing providers. Whichever you choose, the important thing—so important that it may mean the difference between success or failure—is getting access to smart people to help you pull business insight from rapidly filling lakes of data.

Everything you do to build systems of intelligence hinges on your organization's ability to *use* the new raw material of the machine age. Without the talent to do this, every step we outline within this book is moot. Recruit, retrain, contract, acqui-hire, beg, steal, or borrow.[9] The future of your work depends on it.

Build a Halo Business Model

Information begets value, but not without a little help. As we said before, the real key is to simply get started, but at some point you need to show a material ROI.

Virtually every solution we've looked at during the past several years shares the same pattern. Someone had a really rough but interesting idea, and they just started. Even though solutions are different, in all the cases we've investigated, once a business begins to compete with code, the business model emerges.

This may sound easier said than done, but it's happening every day, and it all boils down to establishing the logical link between insight and value. The best advice we ever heard about this is to keep it simple and follow the money.

A large industrial player is now able to commit to very specific savings targets for its customers. A medical-device company now has lower maintenance costs and a streamlined new product development process. Managers of each of these real-world scenarios know that their solutions create real value, and in each case they found a way to monetize that value.

Redesign Your Customer Experiences

Code Halos initially emerged in the world of "consumerized" IT. The members of what we call the Trillion Dollar Club (Google, Amazon, Apple, Facebook, Netflix, and Pandora)[10] were all primarily business-to-consumer, not business-to-business, technology companies. The Web 2.0 movement of the early 2000s led the way in making applications and technology-based services easy on the eye, easy to use, engaging, youthful, and fun, in contrast to "big business" technology, which was (and to a large extent still is) difficult to use and less concerned with making things intuitive and visually attractive.

The Trillion Dollar Club, along with many other companies and organizations (e.g., the social news aggregator Reddit, Twitter, Mashable, microblogging platform Tumblr, room booking app Hotel Tonight), realized that to generate (and keep) users, they needed to simplify the complexity of using technology and compete in markets that increasingly overlapped with the fashion and entertainment industries.

The company that first brought all these trends together was, of course, Apple. Apple realized that the design of a device or an experience—how it looked, how it felt, how it was used, how it was experienced, what feelings and sensations it generated in its user—was no longer something briefly considered by marketers long after engineers had done the *real* work; it was absolutely central to the entire end-to-end process of creating, manufacturing, and selling the device or service.

The success of this philosophy speaks for itself. The beauty of Apple products and the Apple experience has made it the most financially successful company in the history of business. Though "beauty" is an odd, ephemeral, subjective, seemingly non-quantifiable thing, good design has turned out to be the biggest generator of wealth in history. Even the coldest, hardest-hearted, most cynical accountant has to be impressed by that.

The lesson from Apple is that making "things" beautiful is not an esoteric exercise for those with nothing better to do; rather, it is the highest priority on your to-do list. Every example of a successful machine highlighted in this book has a design-thinking approach at its core. Narrative Science, Palantir, New Classrooms, and all the other companies offering systems of intelligence understand that technology for technology's sake is no longer a winning formula.

To build winning machines, you need to have this obsession too. Good design is not a nice-to-have; it's an impossible-without, in *every* aspect of your business. If you're not involving designers from the very beginning of product and services development, you're trying to win a fight with one hand tied behind your back. You're playing an old game when there's a new game in town.

Keep Away from the Dark Side

Once people understand the idea of competing with code, their minds start ticking through the worst-case scenarios of how corporations and governments and hackers can use information provided directly or indirectly (via the metadata of our online activity) to scam, trick, or simply rob us blind. This is the "dark side of the halo."

The thinking behind these dark thoughts is not hard to decipher. The day-to-day news is full of horror stories that show we truly are living in a "world without secrets," as Gartner analyst Richard Hunter put it.[11] In just the past few years, we've seen a raft of high-profile examples of hacking, including the following:[12]

- **Anthem:** 80 million records of current and former customers of the U.S. health insurer were reportedly exposed.
- **Ashley Madison:** 32 million customer accounts of this infamous dating site were accessed.
- **Central Intelligence Agency Director John Brennan:** His personal e-mail account was broken into and details were shared online.
- **The U.S. Government's Office of Personnel Management:** 21 million people's records were hacked, including the fingerprints of 5.6 million federal employees.
- **Sony Pictures:** 47,000 Social Security numbers of employees and contractors were stolen, and e-mails between executives discussing the production and launch of the film *The Interview* were made public.[13]
- **Democratic National Committee (DNC):** 20,000 e-mails from top officials were placed on WikiLeaks.[14]
- **Yahoo:** 500 million customer accounts were hacked.[15]

Not surprisingly, legislators are increasingly focused on wading into these fast-moving and complex waters. The European Union passed a new law—General Data Protection Regulation—in the spring of 2016, encoding the notion of a "right to be forgotten."[16] In the United States, the Federal Bureau of Investigation was facing a Supreme Court showdown over its request that Apple provide information from the iPhone of the San Bernardino shooter until the agency managed to crack into the phone without Apple's assistance.[17]

All this activity and anxiety notwithstanding, the *dark side of the halo* still shows no sign of dampening people's enthusiasm for the *bright side of the halo*. We still continue to vote with our fingers. In the second quarter of 2016, Facebook had 1.7 billion active users per month, up from 1 billion in 2012.[18] At the time of writing, Amazon's market capitalization (around $400 billion) has raced past Walmart's (just over $200 billion), surpassing it for the first time in 2015.[19] Google became the most valuable company on Earth in February 2016.[20] It's clear that—collectively—we place connection, convenience, and insight far above these hacking risks. This is good news for business, because it means we are all getting used to the idea that bad things will happen, but we still expect companies to take sufficient steps to keep us safe because treating data well is the foundation of trust, as shown in Figure 8.2. There are no easy answers, but fortunately, early winners provide some ideas on the rules of the road.

- **Don't be creepy.** The business economics of trust and security are now clear. In our research, we've found that 50% of consumers are ready to pay a premium to do business with companies they trust, and 57% will walk away from companies that have lost their trust (see Figure 8.2).[21] Being very clear about what data you are collecting, why you are collecting it, and what you'll do with it are the first steps to gaining customer trust. Companies have gotten into trouble when they've tried to draw conclusions based on information in a way that leaves customers feeling invaded. We've all felt this when we see an ad for something shortly after a Google search or find our Facebook feed leaking into our ad feed. It doesn't feel right, and more than that, we now know this is shaping brand perceptions.
- **Give your customers a delete button.** A growing number of companies have realized that allowing customers to easily opt out of an information-sharing relationship is a healthy way of giving agency back to all of us, and this helps avoid creating those creepy feelings. Make the delete button easy to find. Hiding it at the end of a labyrinth isn't going to help you win trust points. People give companies data with

DATA IS THE FOUNDATION OF TRUST

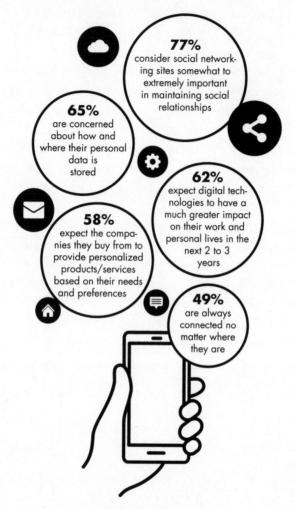

Response base: 2,404 consumers

Source: Cognizant Center for the Future of Work

Figure 8.2   Data Is the Foundation of Trust

an implied or explicit contract, and part of the contract is that we should all be able to walk away with our data. If someone wants out, make sure she can find the exit door easily.

- **Show me you know me.** As data exchanged becomes increasingly informative, companies are able to draw more personal conclusions about each of us. Companies may know if we are prone to driving drunk, have an illness, are getting ready to have a baby, tend to be altruistic, lean to the left or the right politically, and so forth. If a customer asks, "What do you know about me?" you have an obligation to share that information back. *Even if no one ever asks*, you should be ready to be transparent about the kinds of insights you can draw, based on the information you have.

- **Shine a light on the "give-to-get" equation.** Commerce means exchanging value for goods and services, and that doesn't change in a digital economy. Now, however, what's changing hands (or servers) is data. Consumers (or companies) are sharing information for value. We call this the give-to-get relationship. To maintain trust, companies must be explicit about the data being collected and the value being delivered in exchange.
- **Hard-code self-control.** As we noted in *Code Halos*, "Self-regulation by organizations will be a critical element of success." Virtually every major enterprise has loads of content and mountains of policies related to security, privacy, and regulatory compliance. These are decidedly not going away, but they are also insufficient for managing a new economy built on the value of data. In addition, people who will have access to this data will make mistakes. On rare occasions, there may even be a bad actor seeking access to your data for personal gain. What we've learned from forward-thinking companies succeeding in the digital economy is that we need to hard-code self-control. This doesn't mean wrapping yourselves with a protective layer of lawyers and un-implementable processes. It does mean that someone's job should be focused on worrying about data protection, risk exposure, and managing your company's new relationship with data. Because technology outpaces policy, laws and regulations will never catch up. There are no turnkey solutions to risk management, but appointing a chief digital risk officer or amending an existing role to recognize and manage your new risks and responsibilities related to code is a good first step.
- **Breaches will happen, but they are not a death sentence.** Security breaches are now expected, so you should get ready to absorb and manage the inevitable hacks. The targets of the biggest macro-hacks—JMPC, the U.S. Office of Personnel Management, Target, among others—paid a steep price, but virtually all are still open for business.[22] Learn from them: prepare for the dark side of digital, but don't conclude that one adverse event will bring down the company.

Monetize Your Data

Given that data is the raw material for the Fourth Industrial Revolution, it's perhaps no surprise that some companies are now leveraging this proprietary asset by selling it on the market, creating entirely new revenue streams (at enormous margin) that simply didn't exist only a few years ago.

Comcast, for example, has a data "lake" (more like a small sea, actually), full of information on consumers' media consumption habits. This includes data not only on set-top box media but, in many cases, on our browsing habits and more. Comcast is now offering access to its code for a price, because it recognizes that this data is a treasure trove of insight for many other companies.[23]

Iora Health, another company attempting to disrupt the currently dysfunctional U.S. health care system (like TriZetto), is offering a new commercial model based on patient health outcomes, community health coaches, and data management. So far, it's working. By increasing patient engagement, Iora has seen a 35% to 40% reduction in hospitalizations and a 12% to 15% drop in health care costs.[24] In both of these cases, organizations are focusing on data-rich processes and applying new technologies and business models to generate value by monetizing data and accessing *much* larger markets. You should be doing this too.

Digits over Widgets: The Next Age of Business and Technology

Competing with code is now becoming the default model for our modern economy. Instrumenting everything, accessing data scientists and other big data/analytics talent, and avoiding the dark side of the halo are all tactics you must adopt to get started. Fortunes will be won and lost depending on your organization's ability to leverage the upsides of the halo and mitigate its downsides.

In Chapter 7, we showed how automation will be used to cut costs from virtually every business function. That cash must be used to bring Code Halo solutions to life. Winning with data is the number-one competitive game in nearly every industry. Companies that fail to embrace this strategy are destined to come face-to-face with their own extinction event.

Next, we'll explore how systems of intelligence can allow us to be better than we are—smarter, more efficient, more engaged—in short, "enhanced."

9

Enhance

Amplify Human Performance with the New Machine

It's February 2003. You're driving your car to a meeting in downtown Chicago. The traffic is terrible. You're running late. You glance down at the directions and map you've printed out from Yahoo! You know you've got to take Exit 50B from the Kennedy Expressway. You miss it. You take 51B, but then realize it goes west, not downtown. You pull into a gas station, recheck the map, and turn around on Lake Street to get back on the expressway. You miss the turn. You look at your watch: It's 8:55 AM, and the meeting's in five minutes. *"I'm not going to make it; I'm going to mess up the deal; my boss is going to kill me."*

It's February 2017. You're driving your car to a meeting in downtown Chicago. The traffic is terrible. You're running late. From your smartphone, Waze says, "Take North Milwaukee Avenue onto West Grand Avenue." You've never been this way before. A moment later, Waze speaks up again: "Take North Franklin Street, then take East Ohio Street." *"OK,"* you think, *"if you say so."* A couple of minutes go by. "Your destination is on your left in 500 yards." You look at your watch: It's 8:55 AM, and the meeting's in five minutes. *"I'm going to make it; I'm going to close the deal; my boss is going to love me."*

Today, driving places we don't know is so easy, we hardly give it a second thought. Yet, it used to be so tough. Much marital discord, let alone missed sales, stemmed from arguments over whether it was a left or a right at a four-way stop. With smart GPS systems, whether as apps on our smartphones or embedded in our dashboards, it's far more difficult to get lost nowadays. We can now know exactly what to do, when to do it, where to go, what precisely is the next best action, thanks to the miracles of technology enhancement. As a result, many couples have had to find something else to argue about.

The GPS systems we now take for granted provide a preview of coming attractions on how the new machines are enhancing more and more aspects of our work and personal lives. Consider the following choices from your own perspective, as you seek out professionals to assist you in your personal life:

- When ill, would you rather visit a doctor who has tracked all your digital health information, and can, before your visit, juxtapose your information against both your personal history and the exact health trends occurring in your community to make a pinpoint diagnosis? And what if the doctor could then use your time in the office to confirm the diagnosis and discuss your personal path to recovery? Or would you prefer the traditional experience, in which a primary care physician, over the course of a seven-minute visit, pokes and prods you, asks a few questions, then tries to determine your ailment without any assistance in real time, and hands you a prescription while heading out the door?
- In choosing a lawyer, would you prefer one who uses a digital platform to ensure that all the relevant case law—across thousands of cases—has been consulted, and that the full histories of the judge and opposing lawyers are analyzed in preparation for your case? Or would you prefer a lawyer with a small team of paralegals that relies solely on their own skills and personal work experiences to map out your best legal strategy?
- As a parent, would you be more comfortable knowing your child's teacher adjusted the learning plan *every day* to make sure your child was completely on track, or one who could tell you about your child's performance only every few months or so based on the results of a few standardized tests?

When it comes to our own personal choices, the answers become very clear. The vast majority of us will choose to work with the enhanced human, the one who is equipped with a sophisticated system of intelligence at their side.

Additionally, in your professional life, who will your *customers* prefer? The salesperson who is armed to answer every question on product and pricing, or the one who wings it with anecdotes and personality? And in today's war for talent, where will the best employees want to work—where they have the tools to do great work, or where they are still mired in relative drudgery and inefficiency?

For these reasons, we see the forces of enhancement as positive and the concerns over automation-driven job substitution as ill-considered. As we outlined in Chapter 3 ("There Will Be Blood"), the vast majority of white-collar work won't be replaced by these new machines but will be made better with them. We believe that more than 80% of teaching jobs, nursing jobs, legal jobs, and coding jobs will be made more productive, more beneficial, and more satisfying by computers—in other words, *enhanced*.

Stone Age, Bronze Age, Iron Age . . . Digital Age

The story of human evolution is, of course, in many ways the story of our tools, from the sharpened stones used by the *Australopithecus garhi* species in East Africa 2.5 million years ago, to the NVIDIA DIGITS™ DevBox machine used by deep-learning pioneers today. We have used tools to lift ourselves from the savannah to the Sea of Tranquility and in the process, our tools have shaped and dictated the work we do and how we do it.

Tools have always enhanced our human capability. With levers, we can lift far more than we could with our muscles alone. With pistons and gearboxes, we can move more quickly. With calculators, we can add more quickly and accurately than with our brains. With the da Vinci® Surgical System, physicians can now make incisions far less invasively.

Enhancement in the Office

Now our tools are changing again, and therefore, so is our work *and* our human capability. As Joseph Sirosh, corporate vice president of the Data Group at Microsoft, told us, "Pretty much every experience today is made intelligent by data." Pointing to Microsoft's Cortana, an AI-infused digital assistant, Sirosh said, "You will ask questions of Cortana, and it will help you, and it will understand your calendar and understand your meetings. It'll help you be much more efficient. Companies will use the data they have to help their employees succeed better and have healthier lives, manage their own effectiveness at work better, and have better work environments and social structures."

Cortana, in effect, will enhance you as a worker.

This machine intelligence, often packaged anthropomorphically with a human name—also increasingly known as a "bot" or offered simply as a nonhuman computer service—is expanding into an increasingly wider range of tasks and processes, both trivial and profound. While meeting scheduling may still have a "big brains on small things" quality to it, helping doctors diagnose chronic conditions does not.

Enhancement in the Hospital

At the Dartmouth-Hitchcock Medical Center in Lebanon, New Hampshire, Microsoft is working with a multidisciplinary team of doctors and technologists on an initiative called ImagineCare, aimed at enhancing the work of doctors and medical staff with machine intelligence. As Sirosh told us, "It turns out, a lot of chronic conditions—and events associated with chronic conditions—can actually be predicted from data. If a patient has high blood pressure, and is gaining weight, we can predict with fairly high accuracy the risk of the patient having congestive heart failure. And so, if you can predict that, you can avoid that patient being admitted to the emergency room by taking appropriate precautions, such as prescribing diuretics so that the patient doesn't accumulate water in their lungs which leads to the congestive heart failure."

ImagineCare aims to build and expand these predictive services to enhance the work of doctoring, using the new machine and the new raw materials and allowing these machine-driven capabilities to let human competencies scale higher at levels never achievable before.

Enhanced Jobs Will Be Protected Jobs

At the heart of enhancement is the simple idea that nearly every person and job can and must be improved through technology. Every teacher must be an *enhanced* teacher; every banker must be an *enhanced* banker; every soldier must be an *enhanced* soldier. It's you/your job *plus* technology.

Of course, many of us use technology to enhance our work already quite extensively, in a pre-AI way. Take the three of us, for example. We write on computers, talk through videoconferencing machines, read on iPads, and hang out in Google. But even for people seemingly at the cutting edge of technology, there are many aspects of work only marginally touched by technology. New technology could enhance us further: Timesheets and expense reports could be automated; Cortana and Amy could automatically set up our meetings and conference calls; we could use our Alexa-enabled Echo wireless speaker to build a Prezi presentation using just a few spoken word clues: "Get an image of a modern building, and overlay on it the latest quarterly results."[1] The list could go on and on.

For those who see only the downsides of automation, the concept of a *race against the machine*—the phrase coined and popularized by MIT's Erik Brynjolfsson and Andrew McAfee in their book by that title—has become very powerful.[2] But what many people miss is that the authors ultimately pointed out that we're actually in a race *with* the machine.

Technology has always given, and technology has always taken away. Automation and technological substitution of human labor are facts of life. More important, these dynamics are a good thing. More tools mean more leverage, which means more efficiency, which means more productivity. This results in more margin, which means the ability and opportunity to do higher-value work and to use higher-order skills (i.e., to *grow*). This is the route to protecting jobs, not destroying them.

The work of any executive or leader—indeed, of any individual—is, therefore, to identify the roles, processes, systems, and experiences that can be upgraded by newly available technologies and to imagine new approaches and constructs. For a teacher, this might mean "flipping" the school day—doing "homework" in class and doing "class work" such as listening to a lecture, at home. For a banker, this might mean being able to see the financial Code Halo of a customer and knowing instantly what he or she needs next. For a doctor, this might mean seeing the Code Halo of a patient (derived from wearable devices and preexisting medical records) before he or she enters the exam room or, even better, being able to diagnose the patient while the patient is at home. The enhanced teacher or banker or doctor will provide better service, more quickly, at a reduced price (and/or margin) and, in the process, generate all-around improvements (including job security). In this new model, teachers, bankers, and doctors will get back to what they like about their job and slough off the "administrivia" elements that drive them nuts. This is surely a win-win situation for everyone (buyer and seller alike).

These ideas are evident in the ALEKS system from McGraw-Hill Education, mentioned in passing in Chapter 1. ALEKS (**A**ssessment and **LE**arning in **K**nowledge **S**paces) is an online tutoring and assessment program that includes course material in math, chemistry, statistics, and business, aimed at creating tailored and personalized education experiences for each and every individual in a physical classroom or virtual learning environment. As New Classrooms does (discussed in Chapter 2), ALEKS enhances the job of a teacher, making the experience better for the teacher and the students.

You Can't Bring an Apple to ALEKS

McGraw-Hill Education's ALEKS is based on original theoretical work in a field of study called "Knowledge Space Theory." ALEKS dynamically houses and manages "knowledge maps," which continually change based on the learner's interaction. ALEKS takes learners through a course of exploration and mastery, using the knowledge map to establish a pathway and cadence that is personalized to the student's abilities, strengths, and weaknesses.

Stephen Laster, chief digital officer at McGraw-Hill Education, told us that systems like ALEKS "make teaching and learning more engaging, more efficient, and more effective. . . . Imagine you're a community-college professor in a first-year freshman algebra course and you've got 400 students. Better than half of them arrive at your college unprepared, for all the reasons we see in the popular press. What ALEKS allows that teacher to do is, very quickly, through data dashboards and feedback loops, to get a good sense of the class, get a good sense of individual students, and also receive recommendations for sectioning or clumping students together. . . . Could a teacher do that without technology? Sure. Do they have the time to do it? Absolutely not."

The three of us have spent a long time in and around academia and teachers, and we've observed first-hand the incredible dedication required to educate learners of all ages. ALEKS enhances teachers' lives by picking up much of the rote work.

"The value of the teacher isn't sitting there grading or sitting there trying in Excel to create her own analytics or heuristics. We can do that for her," Laster explained. "We can also help her better understand her student. And the value of that teacher is the time she's sitting with students, be it through technology or face-to-face, really providing small-group instruction, providing greater content and all the things that technology can't do well today. That's what ALEKS does for her."

Systems like ALEKS free teachers, in Laster's words, "to think more deeply about the needs of their students. It frees the teacher to spend more time on preparing engaging class experiences, and it frees the teacher to spend more time with her students. Because what ALEKS is doing is relieving her of some of the core grading and analysis that 10 years ago, 15 years ago, she would have had to do by hand on VisiCalc or Excel or what have you. ALEKS allows the teacher to remain in control. She creates her class sessions. She can configure something like ALEKS to her teaching style and the needs of her students. But it's saving her time and allowing her to then focus on those activities that have the biggest impact to her students, which is inspiring them and engaging them."

This is the *enhanced* teacher. This is the teaching profession *protected* by technology, not *replaced* by technology. In fact, the idea of teachers being replaced by "robot tutors in the cloud" is simply a nonstarter for Laster. "The role of the teacher remains central, if not even more important, in a technological age. But it's going to be the role of a mentor. It's the role of spreading wisdom. The teacher as somebody who's requiring you to just learn level one and two, in a rote building blocks way, will decline. That's where technology will have an impact. Teachers have a bright, bright future, though, because learning is inherently social; as you move into the upper grades and into the university and master's levels, it's really about the teacher as the wise guide helping to shape you into the person you've determined you want to be. ALEKS knows its place, and that it works in service of the teacher, in the same way a spreadsheet exists in service of a brilliant finance person."

Figure 9.1   An ALEKS Learning Space

Business and technology leaders looking for lessons on enhancement can learn a lot from McGraw-Hill Education.

- **Get ready to deflate fear of the bots.** The future of work for teachers will be teaching. We are not facing a robot dystopia in which our kids will be taught by bots. Bots will help but not replace teachers. In your own business, follow our Chapter 7 criteria for identifying which types of work should be automated, and then target work that should stay with people but should be enhanced with new technologies like ALEKS. You will need to be ready to explain how enhancement can make life better for more people.
- **Look for opportunities where "real time" makes a real difference.** Systems of intelligence offer both pure processing power and speed. In an educational context, velocity matters a lot. As Laster noted, "When students engage with ALEKS and Connect and LearnSmart, the grading happens almost instantaneously. There's no teacher out there who can grade that frequently." Velocity matters more in some cases than others, but our expectations for instant gratification are higher now than ever. Amazon and others are investing heavily to condense supply chain times to nearly

zero. Imagine what velocity could mean in your own business context. Could enhanced loan processors improve customer satisfaction and revenue by accelerating with technology? How much advantage could you gain if your underwriters could work nearly instantaneously? The point here is that systems of intelligence free up time for higher-value work and improve productivity, which are powerful outcomes of enhancement. The chances are very good that you are sitting on some of these opportunities right now.

- **Aim high and be bold.** Although they came from many different industries and had developed many different kinds of AI platforms, virtually all the builders of the digital economy we met shared almost exactly the same point of view. *None* of them talked about crushing the competition or getting rich. They *all* talked about using technology to solve really important problems in education, health care, agriculture, and a dozen other industries. They all recognized that systems of intelligence are a means to an end, and that creating software for the heck of it is a waste of time and money. As Laster put it, "[Yes], we are about software, and yes, we are about data, but we continue to be about curation, about pedagogy, about how learning happens, about [formative] assessment."

We are not so naïve as to expect good things to happen when you walk into your CEO's office and say, "We shouldn't care about making money; let's just invest heavily in making the world a better place." Candidly, that's just bad strategy. One of the things we can learn from McGraw-Hill Education is to be bold within the context of your brand and the services you are selling. That *is* fair game for enhancement solutions in the digital economy.

Smart Robots Make Smarter Hands

The combination of "smart hands" and "smart robots" is becoming more visible all the time, and not only does the machine continually get smarter (as we have outlined previously in the book), but so does the human. A great example of this is buried within one of the most widely known moments of this new man/machine relationship, when world Go champion Lee Sedol competed against Google's AlphaGo AI machine.

In their 2016 match, AlphaGo made a move—Move 37—that surprised Sedol (and all the expert commentators); in fact, it was considered a mistake by the Google team. It turned out, however, to be the winning move in game two of the five-game series. In game four, Sedol made a move—Move 78—that surprised AlphaGo, because as Demis Hassabis, cofounder of DeepMind, the team behind AlphaGo, put it, "AlphaGo didn't think a human would ever play it."[3] With Move 78, Sedol won game four.

Although AlphaGo went on to win the series-deciding fifth game, Sedol reflected afterward that he wouldn't have been able to make Move 78 unless he had played against AlphaGo; it had "opened his eyes" to new ways of playing the game. Sedol had, in effect, been enhanced; he became smarter and more sophisticated through his interaction with the machine.

The Machine as Coach

Countering the notion that machines will render large sectors of the bourgeois workforce obsolete, Max Yankelevich, founder and CEO of smart process automation vendor WorkFusion, sees a much more nuanced future ahead. As he told us, "The combination of a human plus AI will see one plus one equal three. . . . Our customers are not looking to get rid of their people; they're actually looking to move them up to more revenue-generating activities that are more intellectually challenging. They see AI as an opportunity to move their people up the intellectual stack, where they become more productive contributors to the enterprise. That's how we see things evolving."

In the way that AlphaGo made Lee Sedol a better Go player, machines working side-by-side in the trenches of enterprise work will make us better at what we do. And not just in the most elite types of work, such as performed by doctors and lawyers, but also in the prosaic, unglamorous work carried out every day in millions of cubicles all around the world: the work of processing an insurance claim, of handling a customer complaint, of making sure widget A gets from point B to C.

WorkFusion's software, which is used by enterprise businesses to digitize processes such as customer on-boarding, trade settlements, and claims processing, automates a wide variety of routine knowledge work through robotics and machine learning—what WorkFusion refers to as cognitive automation. Robotics automates the purely rules-driven work of operating legacy applications and moving structured data from system to system, and cognitive automation tackles judgment work performed on more complex, unstructured data. The software learns through a combination of historical data and by "watching" workers categorize and extract unstructured data in real time. Initially, humans validate Work-Fusion's output, but as the number of process repetitions grows from hundreds to thousands, the software can perform autonomously, and it automatically escalates exceptions that need full human judgment. As Yankelevich puts it, "Automation performs that high-volume, routine work, and humans handle the more interesting and more challenging type of work, but lower volumes of it."

Yankelevich's vision, though, is definitely to "keep humans in the loop" and to leverage the power of machines to create work that is more valuable, both for organizations and for people. Yankelevich firmly believes that smart process automation is the route not just to cost savings but to better types of work. Yankelevich describes it as "work requiring the human touch, really expert type of work, work that requires a lot of different thought processes and is intellectually challenging, and which allows us, as societies, to become more productive in the creative areas."

Though for many the story of automation, AI, and machines centers solely on "destruction," the "creative" forces that machines unleash will be their real legacy. Unlike in the world of tennis where Andy Murray's coach, former world number one Ivan Lendl, would struggle to get his ideas across to somebody with a 3.0 rating at the local club, the algorithms in smart process-automation software are far more democratic, helping every level of worker to level-up. WorkFusion software can elevate both a Harvard-educated lawyer and a community college-educated clerk by automating the work that keeps them both from higher-value contribution. This is the real power of the machine in a world where machines are getting smarter, not to replace us, but to help us get higher up the rankings into bigger tournaments with bigger prize money.

This man/machine relationship, along with the human work enhancement it creates, can also be understood through the work of Amazon engineers, who use the machine-learning capabilities being developed within Amazon Web Services (AWS).

Dr. Matt Wood, general manager of product strategy at AWS, explained to us, "We ran a little test internally where we had two senior developers try to predict a customer's gender, just using their name. The way you would traditionally do this is to look at census data and say, 'Well, the majority of people called Matt turn out to be male,' and build predictive models around that." The engineers found, however, that there were some gray areas: "If you have a Pat or a Sam, it's harder to identify gender based on that," Wood said. The two engineers went off to solve this challenge, building algorithms from scratch. It took them almost two months to build the software and validate it and train the models, according to Wood, but after two months, they got to over 90% accuracy with their predictions. "'Pretty good job,' we thought," Wood recounted. "Then we took a single developer on a different team, and we gave them the pre-developed AWS internal machine-learning service, and they, too, got to the same level of accuracy, over 90% accuracy, but they were able to do it *in a matter of days*."

Wood believes that "in the fullness of time, the majority of challenges will be addressed through a machine-learning component. It will play a role in a very, very large number of use cases and challenges that customers are facing."

Wood anticipates that more experts will interact with machine-learning platforms over time. In pairing smart people with systems that have large (and rapidly expanding) collections of data, these enhanced people will deliver value that scales and grows in sophistication over time.

As Wood put it, "You have this nice kind of virtuous cycle of the development, method-usage, data creation, and problem-solving, which flows back into creating more data, then flows back into the various ways in which you may choose to optimize a particular approach or method, and the cycle just keeps going around and around."

Using our new tools to enhance our work will help us reach the next level of human performance. And frankly, there's a lot to enhance.

Enhancement Is Technology in Service to the Human

One important but often overlooked aspect of enhancing work is to recognize the relationship that exists between enhancing a job/role/process and automating it. In many ways, automation and enhancement exist in a symbiotic, two-sides-of-the-same-coin way. To effectively enhance, one needs to automate. The teacher is afforded the opportunity to "flip" the classroom only if he or she automates aspects of the learning and teaching workflow. If the teacher doesn't automate the lesson, then there is no way to free up the time during the day to attend to each individual student's particular requirements. If the banker doesn't automate the creation of the customer's Code Halo, he or she will spend the whole time, which could be spent with the customer developing the relationship *in a human way*, collating all the information needed to build that full view of a customer. Automation is not the enemy of enhancement; it is, in fact, central to the ability to enhance in the first place.

In the next wave of competitive battle—at a commercial, societal, economic level—the winners will be those who continue to believe in the progress created by technology, those who enhance, those who understand the power of "tools" and who adapt to using them effectively.

What to Do on Monday? Partner with Systems of Intelligence

There are two major steps you can take today (whether or not it's Monday) to get the enhance ball rolling:

1. Double-down on being more human.
2. Build your white-collar exoskeleton.

Double-Down on Being More Human

The more technology enhances us, the more it creates the opportunity for a human touch. When the computer does what it does well, it allows us to focus more on what we do well: being empathetic, building relationships, and making sense of complex situations.

Think of the last time you went to a rental-car counter at the airport. After getting off your long and cramped flight and standing in line at the rental agency for 15 minutes, you finally get to a customer service representative. Were you met with a warm and welcoming greeting, followed by a quick yet thoughtful discussion of your plans, your car needs, your specific rental, and options? Or did the service agent acknowledge your presence with a grunt, followed by no eye-contact or conversation as he stared into his computer, entering information and clicking through menus for several minutes before producing a three-page contract in triplicate? The three of us travel a lot, so we know the answer: there's a 90% chance it was the latter.

In the case of the rental-car agent as well as thousands of similar roles and processes across all industries, we don't blame the employee; we blame the company. After all, the company hasn't armed this customer-facing associate to do his job properly—to be, well, human. Instead, he's been saddled with burdensome technology that, after eight hours a day, has bludgeoned the good humor out of him. Instead of getting to the essence of his job—of being the friendly face of the company and ensuring the happiness of a customer— he spends most of his time managing cumbersome systems layered on an archaic process.

This is just one type of situation that can be made more human with the new machine. As next-generation technology relieves this customer service agent's workload, requiring no more manual entry in a system of record, he will be liberated to provide a truly human touch.

We now see this in many sectors of retail, including:

- **Zappos**, the leading shoe e-tailer, for years has been leveraging its customer-service department. While Zappos may seem like a tech-first company, it long ago recognized that when customers reached out by calling its call center, it was the company's chance to cement a customer relationship. And how far will Zappos go? One particular call lasted 10 hours and 29 minutes! The vast majority of that call wasn't about shoes at all, but the customer's interest in life in the Las Vegas area. The Zappos reaction? "Sometimes people just need to call and talk. We don't judge; we just want to help." Oh, and yes, the customer did end up purchasing a pair of UGG boots.[4]
- At **Pret A Manger**, a quickly growing, high-end, fast-food retail chain, the majority of the food selection in its stores is done by self-service, and the point-of-sale checkout is seamless. But the personality of Pret A

Manger is not based on this combination of high-quality food sold efficiently and at a good price. The cornerstone of the customer experience is its floor staff, who are quirky, fun, and engaged. By driving efficiencies in certain parts of its operations, Pret has doubled-down on being more human, in giving customers not just quality food but also an upbeat and positive break in their busy, stressful workdays.[5]

- **Apple** has similarly changed the game in retail by radically altering the point-of-sale experience, eliminating checkout counters, and putting automated tools in the hands of its floor staff. With all this automation, what did Apple do? The company doubled-down on more blue-shirted staff who are available to consult with customers, and provide a real sense of humanity in a company mostly selling silicon and bits.[6]

As shown in these examples, more enhancement actually allows for more humanity.

Where do such opportunities reside in your company? Start by looking at those customer "moments of truth." For Zappos, it was when an online order went wrong. At Pret A Manger, it was when a busy customer simply wanted to grab a sandwich very quickly without being snarled up with other customers' more complicated orders. And for Apple, it was when one of their nontechnical customers felt overwhelmed by their powerful machines. In looking for the human touch, don't just look for moments that are easy. Instead, look to those that are hard, when you truly solve a customer problem with a sense of service and a generosity of spirit.

In an enhanced world of more pervasive technology, activities that humans do well will become even more important in 2020 than today. Analytical, communication, and learning skills as well as the ability to relate to other people have always been and will remain vital for business success. In our recent study of 2,000 global business leaders, respondents said that in the coming years, these very human traits—things we do naturally but that computers can hardly accomplish—will become even more essential in our personal and work lives and for our businesses (see Figure 9.2).

All of us, bosses included, need to enhance our current skills when it comes to engaging with others: leading, reasoning and interpreting, applying judgment, being creative, and applying the human touch. These behaviors and activities are still far outside the purview of current and near-future technologies and will remain so for years to come, even as the new machines become more capable.

SKILLS YOU'LL NEED TO IMPROVE TO STAY RELEVANT IN THE FUTURE
By 2020, senior executives project that employees will need to improve their performance in these areas:

Analytical Thinking **21%**

Social Media **15%**

Fabrication Skills **15%**

Learning **14%**

Inclusion **13%**

Written Communication **13%**

Interpersonal Skills **12%**

Language Skills **12%**

Global Operating **12%**

Response base: 2,000 senior business leaders
Source: Cognizant Center for the Future of Work.

Figure 9.2   Beat the Bot by Being a Better Human

Major companies today are proving that even in a world of enhancement solutions, where people and machines work together in new ways, there's still value in being human. Our work ahead will require us to double-down on the activities where humans have and will continue to have an advantage over silicon.

Build Your White-Collar Exoskeleton

The idea of enhancing our human capabilities with technology has been the dream of science fiction for many years. In the late 1950s, Robert Heinlein imagined teams of soldiers enhanced with armored exoskeletons in *Starship Troopers*. Over 30 years later in the movie *Aliens*, Warrant Officer Ellen Ripley used a Power Loader to defend a colonist from the Alien Queen, high above the planet LV-426 (as shown in Figure 9.3).

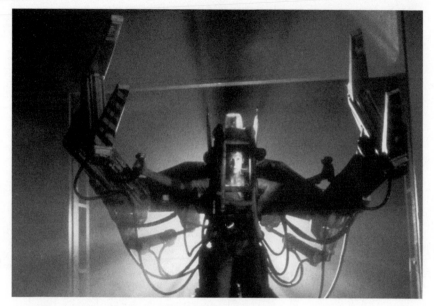

Figure 9.3   Ripley and Her Front Loader

These science fiction speculations are increasingly losing their classification as fiction; now, they are becoming fact. The idea of an "exoskeleton" is, indeed, an inspiration for a number of new technologies that assist with both physical and intellectual work.

For example, Sarcos, a U.S. developer of robotics and micro-electro-mechanical systems, has built a prototype exoskeleton for military personnel to enhance their physical capabilities in the field. Panasonic has developed a line of exoskeletons designed to help workers lift heavy items without straining their backs.[7] Ekso Bionics, a company spun out of the University of California's Robotics and Human Engineering Laboratory at Berkeley, has created the first FDA-approved exoskeleton that gives major stroke and spinal cord injury sufferers the ability to walk again.

Figure 9.4 shows Amanda Boxtel walking with the help of an Ekso Bionics exoskeleton suit. Amanda is a paraplegic, having sustained a spinal cord injury from a skiing accident more than two decades ago in 1992, and is unable to walk on her own.

Physical exoskeletons point the way to how we can overcome our limitations and frailties. Exoskeletons designed to enhance our minds rather than our bodies may not be as visually arresting as body suits and body armor,

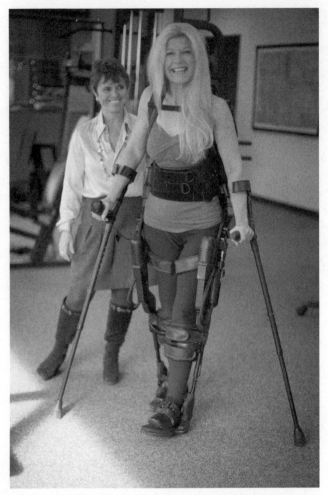

Figure 9.4   Amanda Boxtel with Her Exoskeleton

but they ultimately may have more impact in terms of taking human performance to the next level.

Palantir Technologies is a leader in providing exoskeletons for the brain. Founded in 2004 with funders including In-Q-Tel, the VC-arm of the U.S. Central Intelligence Agency, Palantir has traditionally worked with defense and security agencies to identify criminals and terrorists. The firm has always been about enhancement; it states, "We build products that make people better at their most important work—the kind of work you read about on the front page of the newspaper, not just the technology section."

More recently, the firm has begun applying its expertise to commercial pursuits, such as the detection of unauthorized trading.

In conjunction with Credit Suisse, Palantir has formed a joint venture, Signac, to monitor trading activity in investment banks and identify patterns of behavior indicative of unlawful trading. Signac collects data from employees and external events and runs this information through Palantir's systems of intelligence (which also rely heavily on trained analysts to extract conclusions). The intent is to stop policy breaches and protect the bank's assets and brand.

It's now becoming apparent that humans alone, unless they are enhanced, simply can't keep up with intelligent automation systems for some tasks. An example is the field of radiology, which is ripe for enhancement.[8] In fact, radiologists will soon be able to "partner" with systems such as IBM's Avicenna to improve diagnostic accuracy. The software—in another great example of a system of intelligence—is being designed to pull together massive amounts of data from the patient's family history, medical imaging, additional test results, and text notes and run it all through an AI machine that helps provide the radiologist with valuable insight.[9] The average radiologist reads 20,000 films a year; given the catastrophic repercussions of missing something, the idea of being enhanced, not replaced, will offer tremendous benefits.

Whether it's education, health care, or financial services, a common theme runs across all the examples given in this chapter: finding a specific business process and applying a system of intelligence to that work in a way that creates a knowledge economy exoskeleton around skilled employees and associates. Similar to the approach we suggest for automation initiatives, you should start with activities that are high-volume and data-rich and that follow a generally recurring process (such as claims adjudication, identifying data patterns, etc.).

You + New Tools = Enhancement

We are in an incredible time, when technology is significantly extending the envelope of human capability. Systems of intelligence now allow us to do things at a level of productivity and profitability that even a few years ago would have seemed far-fetched and implausible.

All of these possibilities and many more are being created by the injection of intelligence into our tools. We have the potential to become smarter because our tools are becoming smarter. This is an important point to realize. It would be extremely arrogant to think that humans today are any smarter than Aristotle or Shakespeare—or Steve Wozniak. But our tools are. And, of course, it's our tools that are really at the heart of the progress we've made so far and the progress we'll make ahead.

Enhancement will be the force that causes the bar to rise for every one of us, in every organization and in every country in the world. If you can enhance the value you generate, you are doing the right things as machines begin to do everything. Enhancement also introduces new avenues of opportunity that we need to explore to keep ahead. Down one of these avenues, you'll soon bump into the next letter of our AHEAD model: A for *abundance*.

10 | Abundance

Finding Your 10X Opportunities with the New Machine

The concept of abundance is really quite simple: as prices go down, demand goes up. We learn this in the first week of Economics 101.

Although AI-generated abundance is new, the underlying idea of abundance is actually quite old; it has been a hallmark and productivity driver of every preceding phase of industrial growth. The loom led to abundance in clothing, the steam engine to abundance in transoceanic travel, and the assembly line to an abundance of refrigerators finding their way into homes all around the world. Before the revolutions that spurred them, these products were rare luxuries. Afterward, they were democratized and ubiquitous.

With systems of intelligence in play, we will soon experience a new wave of abundance, in areas such as financial services, insurance, health care, entertainment, and education. As the new machine drives price points down, markets of abundance will be established, driving sales up to unimagined levels.

The question now becomes: Will your organization seize advantage with the new abundance or fall victim to it?

Microsoft's Joseph Sirosh told us he sees this abundance emerging in health care, with new levels of individualized delivery: "You can say now if you are going to keep people healthier using data and predictive analytics, you will need fewer nurses and doctors and interim-care patients. . . . That sounds like labor substitution. But, what you are getting in return is a very large population that is leading healthier, happier lives [and who] can be productive and creative and contributing [more] to the whole economic engine."

During the past century, we have used raw materials, new machines, and innovative business models to create unprecedented abundance and democratize luxury with physical goods. Now, as abundance markets open up in the digital economy, there are dozens of areas across knowledge-based industries in which the machine will do almost everything. But at the same time, we're seeing the impact of digital abundance in the physical world, as well (remember, hybrid is the new black). A good example of this is Narayana Health, which is using the new machine to bring a form of abundance to those in need of heart surgery.

A Hundred Times More Heart

Narayana Health (NH), launched in 2000 by Dr. Devi Shetty in Bengaluru, India, is revolutionizing cardiac surgery by leveraging digital technology. In the process of doing so, the organization has saved hundreds of thousands of lives over the past decade and a half. By lowering the cost of heart surgery approximately a hundred-fold, Dr. Shetty and his team have delivered the remarkable gift of abundance to patients in India. In a part of the world where heart disease had previously been a death sentence, NH now provides world-class heart surgeries to anyone in need.

Since its inception, NH has grown to 54 facilities, employing over 2,600 full-time doctors and 13,500 people in total, and now treats more than two million patients a year.[1] This abundance-based growth is not in some e-business with no moving parts, but in the most physically intensive of fields possible, built one open-heart surgery at a time. What has accounted for such rapid growth?

By applying the new machine to all of the processes before and after a patient is in the operating room, NH can now provide bypass surgery at an average cost of approximately $1,200.[2] (Consider that the average price tag in the United States for this procedure is usually more than $100,000.)[3] In addition to its dramatically lower costs, NH's mortality and infection rates are the same as those in North America and Europe.[4] No wonder *The Wall Street Journal* refers to Dr. Shetty as "the Henry Ford of heart surgery."[5]

These results are delivered neither by magic nor by cutting corners. Yes, there are salary disparities between India and other countries, but these account for only a fraction of the cost difference. The vast majority of these dramatic savings come from the digitization of key processes. When they launched NH, Dr. Shetty and his team looked at every process associated with heart surgery and viewed it as being hybrid. Some portions must of course remain highly physical—human-centric work performed by medical professionals on an actual patient—whereas others can be significantly digitized, such as monitoring patients and machines.

For example, NH has completely rethought and retooled the intensive-care unit by applying digital technology. The team driving the change took a traditional, paper-based management model and deployed new technologies to a very physical set of work processes. Now, nearly everything is sensor-enabled—patients, medical equipment, nurses, and so forth—and is continually monitored across more than 150 parameters covering vitals, ventilators, labs, nursing tasks, infusions, and orders. The average patient generates approximately 5 GB of data per day (equivalent to about 2,000 e-mails or 900 minutes of YouTube videos). The data is also configured for protocols and requirements specific to different specialties, regions, and hospitals. This instrumentation also provides analytical insights on the effectiveness of doctors and nurses.

By breaking down the processes of surgery prep, operating-room management, and intensive-care-unit operations into discrete processes and experiences and then applying new technologies, NH cut costs to the point that it now can provide high-quality care to many more people. In this instructive, as well as heartwarming, case study, digital is literally saving lives.

In the coming pages, we'll outline how you can find digital abundance in your company. The low-hanging fruit, the easiest abundance opportunities to find and implement, will be in areas of the business that can be readily and fully digitized, such as robo-advisory finance. However, as seen in the NH example, even the most physical activities can be completely rethought and re-architected with the application of the new machine.

Moore's Law Is Bringing Abundance to Your Business

Examples like Narayana Health are evidence, as we see it, of a wide-scale trend. As core processes become instrumented and digitized, entirely new thresholds of price, quality, and customization are being created for customers. This phenomenon is at the center of the success and scale of both Spotify and WeWork, for example, as these companies create abundance by automating the matching of supply and demand in their respective markets.

But what organizations such as NH, Betterment, and Airbnb have all learned is that setting a new price point is not a one-time thing. Instead, it is a continual process. Why? Because once automation takes hold of your product's innards—that is, as their creation and delivery transition from being human-based to machine-based—they will become inherently tech-centric, and thus able to benefit from the power of Moore's Law. This foundational building block of the tech industry has been the bedrock of innovation and affordability for decades, but hasn't had an effect on the cost of insurance policies, doctor's visits, or educational tutoring services, which all cost about the same as they did 20 years ago.

That's about to change, however, as many products and services become digital to the core. As we described in Chapter 7 (on automation), your knowledge processes are about to become radically more efficient. When automation is focused on internal processes, you can achieve substantial savings. And when automation is focused on your products and services, the benefits should accrue to your customers in the form of abundance.

As product managers in Silicon Valley plan for products two years out that are double the performance and/or half the cost, you should now be thinking along similar lines with your information-based products and services. We realize it can be intimidating to look at your best-selling products and services and think, "Those will have to cost less than half their current price in five years," but such is the competitive challenge in the new machine age.

What to Do on Monday? Find Abundance in Your Organization

At this stage, you may wonder how exactly to kick-start momentum toward acting on the idea of abundance. Here are seven approaches that we've seen deliver positive results:

1. Obsess about the start-up community.
2. Kill your company.
3. Play the "tomorrow it's free" game.
4. Manage your innovator's dilemma.
5. Make like a maker.
6. Think like a corner shop (new personalization).
7. Apply digital Taylorism.

Obsess About the Start-Up Community

FinTech, HealthTech, InsuranceTech, LawTech, and GovTech.

These industry movements all have abundance at their core. They are well funded. And those launching these industry disruptors are more than happy to talk about themselves.

Make sure you and your colleagues are listening.

To that end, you should have a team focused exclusively on the new companies that are coming after your business. It doesn't really matter where such a group is placed; we have seen this role inside the strategy function, in R&D, under the chief digital officer, or within IT. The key is that this team should be empowered to take an objective view of the tech-based companies that are looking to bring abundance to your industry and potentially to eat your lunch in the process.

Have this team draw up a "market map," which examines all the offers your company provides and juxtaposes them against the start-up community. For each offer, the team should determine how many start-ups exist in that space, how much money has been invested in them (and by whom), and the maturity and customer-count of such firms. The team should update the map on a quarterly basis, because such a dynamic view will very clearly expose which new ideas are gaining customer traction.

When done properly, such market maps will provide you with a clear picture of threats and opportunities. For example, there may be a dozen start-ups clumped around one of your core products. In this case, Silicon Valley clearly is coming for that portion of your company, and you need to marshal an appropriate response right away—whether it be to buy, to build, or to partner to address the threat.

Similarly, such market maps can save you a lot of heartache by avoiding failed initiatives. When it comes to abundance, there are more failures than successes. OPM (i.e., "other people's money") R&D is the best form possible. Let others waste their money and time in learning that a certain abundance idea won't work.

The key to this dedicated team's success is to grant them true objectivity in both organization and orientation. Allow them to ask dumb questions. Liberate them from hidebound orthodoxies; in times of new abundance, good companies go bad when established managers are constrained by tradition. (Just ask the former teams from Blockbuster or Kodak or Nokia.) Initially, a new offer will nearly always look inferior, flawed, or irrelevant. Your more experienced managers, who grew up with traditional industrial offers, may be dismissive of proposed abundance offers. They'll find scenarios in which they won't work (and will often point to issues such as channel conflict, security, or regulation). To save your abundance team from such constrained thinking, it's vitally important to provide them with the right structure, incentives, and (when necessary) protection to keep the company on the cutting edge in times of change.

Ask Your Sharpest Employees to Kill Your Company

Perspective matters. You have employees—sometimes millennials younger than 32 along with others who simply have fresh thinking—who can offer a unique and highly valuable point of view regarding your traditional industrial-model company. As a best practice, ask a group of them to build a company killer. That's right: ask them for ideas on how to put your company out of business.

In many ways, forward-leaning associates are living in a parallel universe, which we call the "Sunday night, Monday morning" phenomenon. That is, on Sunday night they are using digital platforms to manage their personal affairs—entertaining themselves, connecting with friends, shopping, and handling their households and finances, often all at the same time. Their smartphones truly are the remote controls for most of their lives. Then, when they arrive at work some eight hours later, they must reenter the old physical world, supporting an organization that has been operating as it has been for decades.

This Sunday/Monday dichotomy can be both jarring and frustrating for these employees, as they (rightfully) ask, "Why can't work be as seamless, friction-free, and engaging as my home life?" They know one is the future, the other the past.

To that end, instead of letting these associates wallow in frustration, ask them to architect the future. Specifically, ask them to come up with five new tech-based products or services that would put your company out of business. You might be surprised with how quickly (and passionately) they come up with their suggestions.

Play the "Tomorrow It's Free" Game

Look at your company's most expensive, premium-level, differentiated products and services. Now imagine them at 10% of the market price. Scary? No doubt, given that you've just imagined a hollowed-out revenue stream. It's concerning, but this increasingly common development is what you need to prepare for; if it can happen in heart surgery, it can happen anywhere.

Playing "tomorrow it's free" isn't so much of a glib game as a serious exercise in setting strategy around abundance markets. This means leadership must ask hard, even painful, questions about the implications of current products and services moving from expensive and rare, to cheap and nearly ubiquitous.

Engaging in this experiment will introduce real risks and challenge long-standing orthodoxies. In the life-sciences industry, for example, imagine *all* your drugs and devices off patent. Imagine more of your therapies tailored to an individual's genome (sensitive to our specific DNA, epigenome, microbiome, and virome).[6] How can you use information to create more value associated with your high-priced compounds? How can you leverage systems of intelligence to create new ecosystems of offerings around such bespoke medicines? These are the kinds of questions you and your teams should be asking.

And what happens if you're in retail? If so, you're already living through the new Amazon epoch. You know that people still want to go to a physical store, but imagine if nobody bought anything there ("showrooming" at an exponential level). How can you continue to create a sticky customer experience with new machines? How can you grow your digital revenue from single digits to double digits over the next few years? Some retailers are already making bold moves along these lines. Walgreens, for example, is using a conjunction of technology and its physical retail presence to begin offering lower-cost, high-volume health care.[7]

Of course, nothing will truly be free; one way or another, you need to find ways to grow revenue. Yet we have found this exercise to be healthy, for it breaks associates from their ingrained supply-based thinking. Most of us (consciously or unconsciously) conceive of our companies' products or services as the sum of their parts, which all adds up to a certain price. When we are forced to completely flip this perspective to demand-side thinking (and even very selfish, "I want it for free" thinking), completely new perspectives can arise. If you're not looking at your current portfolio of products and services and playing the "tomorrow it's free" game, prepare to be surprised, because your competitors known and unknown certainly are.

Manage Your Innovator's Dilemma

The strategy of building products or services that you sell at one-tenth the cost of your existing offerings is not without its challenges. Chief among them is the question of how such prospective products or services—priced very differently, aimed at very different customer segments, and entailing very different economics and management models of production, distribution, and margins—coexist within the same overall portfolio of market offerings? Frequently asked questions of this approach include:

- How can we make a profit if we drop our prices 90%?
- Won't we cannibalize our existing market?

- Do we have the right brand to operate in new markets?
- Do we have the right people, with the right skills, to operate in low-cost markets?

Such concerns are well-founded and on point. Moving into abundance-based markets *is* nontrivial. In fact, perhaps the most influential business book of the past 20 years—*The Innovator's Dilemma,* by Harvard Business School professor Clayton M. Christensen—tackles exactly this challenge, although it was written in 1997 before software really began eating the world and does not expressly address disruption created by platforms and cloud computing, let alone systems of intelligence.

Inspired by Christensen and refined by our work with clients, we have identified three key concepts that are effective in handling these challenges:

1. **The Three Horizons Model:** Initially popularized by McKinsey & Co., the Three Horizons Model (THM) recognizes the need to separate an overall business into three distinct parts focused on whether they address the immediate concerns of today's market, the market's needs in the short-term future, or those over a longer time period (hence three horizons).[8] The model aligns the right resources (staffing, ROI expectations, management metrics, etc.) to the right horizon; there is no point, for example, in expecting a new service operating in a nascent market niche to yield the same fat profit margin that a well-established service in a mature market commands. Derivations of this approach include Gartner's Bimodal IT strategy, which structures the IT function into two groupings, one focused on "legacy" technology and one on "next-generation" technology.

2. **The Ellison-Benioff Model:** At the dawn of the cloud computing wave, Oracle co-founder Larry Ellison invested $2 million in his youngest-ever vice president Marc Benioff's start-up, Salesforce.com.[9] Benioff had been trying to convince Ellison that cloud computing was an important trend but Ellison remained unmoved, seeing only the complexities of managing an inherently "anti-Oracle" idea within his core business.[10] Instead, Ellison became Benioff's initial seed investor, wished him well, and watched as his investment blossomed into a $450 million holding in Salesforce. Funding external start-ups to pursue abundance-based models short-circuits many of the intra-business unit problems associated with developing a disruptive idea within a large company.

3. **The LVMH Model:** French holding company LVMH Moët Hennessy Louis Vuitton SE manages more than 60 subsidiary companies that operate independently within its umbrella.[11] Although some back-office functions are shared across the different companies—including many famous brands, such as Bulgari (jewelry, watches, and luxury goods); TAG Heuer (watches); Fendi (luxury fashion); and Thomas Pink (luxury clothing)—they all, for the most part, pursue their individual markets in their own ways. The LVMH model does not try to squeeze disparate products, which often have overlapping market segments, into neatly confined niches, nor does the company attempt to address competitive tensions between its different brands. The LVMH approach, which has become increasingly influential in recent years, allows the company's various subsidiaries to approach the market in differing ways. New ideas find room to breathe within this structure.

Make Like a Maker

One source of inspiration and talent focused on leveraging abundance is the "maker" movement.[12] Growing organically as a subculture within technology circles in recent years, the movement comprises individuals, teams, and companies enthusiastic about building new devices (and tinkering with existing ones) that live at the intersection of new functionality and low cost. For example, makers take old crafts such as woodworking or metalworking and mix those with new skills around 3-D printing and robotics to reassert the value of *making* things rather than just *using* things made by big multinationals in faraway places.

Makers are typically engineers (professional and amateur) by background and entrepreneurial in spirit, and are often at a point in their careers when they're not fully "out on their own" with their pet idea or their true work. We find many such makers on our travels working in big companies who, while holding down their day job, are itching to really focus on their weekend avocation. Don't look upon such individuals as uncommitted to the work at hand; rather, harness their talents, energy, and passions by putting them in places and positions in which their personal innovations can become your corporate innovations.

If Steve Wozniak's Apple 1 had been a Hewlett-Packard product in 1976, the entire history of the high-technology industry would likely have been very different.[13] Many companies are already sponsoring "maker spaces" within their communities for civic reasons, but they are more fully embracing makers as part of an innovation ecosystem and as an important (and cost-effective) way of sourcing abundance-related ideas that otherwise would likely be invisible.

Think Like a Corner Shop: The New Personalization

A dramatically lower price point is only one threshold of abundance. A second and equally important touchstone is greatly increased personalization.

In much the same way that the proprietor of the old corner shop knew the personal needs and quirks of all his customers, the new abundance affords you the same opportunity. This is not a function of scale; after all, look to the personalization Facebook provides its 1.7 billion users. It's simply a function of applying the new machine to establishing one-to-one connections with your customers.

It's easier said than done for 100-year-old companies. Industrial companies have been fantastic at the one-to-many business model. After all, that was their goal, and their entire value chains and customer value propositions were focused on this pursuit. Mercedes delivers top-end quality in all of its automobiles. Marriott offers a consistent lodging experience for its business travelers, regardless of location.

But one-to-many product capability is now table stakes. The new competitive battleground is focused on truly being one-to-one and thereby unearthing new abundance Thus, the individualized capabilities outlined in Chapter 8 on Halos are central to the new abundance.

As we noted earlier, personalization is now the new battleground in the athletic apparel industry. Under Armour has burst onto the scene to become a tier-one competitor with Nike and Adidas. Now it is looking to go further, by leveraging technology to provide one-to-one experiences with its customers. Said CEO Kevin Plank:

> *Imagine you're traveling in Chicago for work. You went for a run one morning, and you had a cold the day before. It's 7 degrees in Chicago, so I know your nose was probably running the whole time. Well, we make this great run glove—we call it the snot finger glove, because it's got basically a microfiber personal Kleenex attached to*

it so you can rub your nose. Imagine if I could send you an ad that says, "Hey, are you going to be in Chicago for another day? Would you like us to send you a pair of gloves?"[14]

Knowing just when and where you need the snot finger glove—now *that's* one-to-one personalization that can open up entirely new abundance markets.

Apply "Digital Taylorism"

New abundance is, first and foremost, all about finding dramatic cost savings to open new markets. How best to find these breakthroughs? By tying the new technologies of AI to the old management principle of Taylorism (a concept we first broached in Chapter 6).

A century ago, industrialized societies became obsessed with measurement in an effort to drive efficiencies and boost quality in the manufacturing process. The father of the management consulting industry, Frederick Winslow Taylor, introduced the idea of scientific management to the early 20th century industrial production line with his book *The Principles of Scientific Management.* [15] Taylor advanced the idea that almost every work activity in a factory could and should be broken down into discrete tasks and measured in time, motion, and output. More important, performance levels and best practices could be codified and replicated. Such thinking became foundational to the industrial model, driving new levels of coordination, output, and quality.

At the time, some decried Taylorism, pointing to what they saw as its dehumanization and removal of the individual decision-making of traditional craftsmen. But economics ultimately won out; Taylor's ideas led to a global trend, and the scientific decomposition of work allowed industrial best practices to spread far and wide, across industries and geographies.

Today's hyper-instrumented and analyzed world is taking Taylorism to entirely new levels. Knowledge work can be studied and optimized in the way industrial work was a century ago. This will have far-reaching implications for the future of your work and for the competitiveness of your company.

Digital Taylorism's ideas are particularly important for digitally focused innovations within large organizations. Innovation is inherently messy, but it needn't be chaotic. Many companies attempt to lower costs to expand markets, but many initiatives fail because of a sense of "ownership." The mandate to "think differently" is something, we've often seen, that goes missing in action. The rigor and metrics associated with digital Taylorism seem to become sacrificed to a loosening of the conventional business disciplines that hold sway in the established parts of the business. Insisting on applying the highest standards of organizational and process best practices from the era of Taylor to our digital economy can help organizations inject a philosophy of standardization and continuous improvement into their digital efforts.

Increasing Prosperity by Lowering Prices

Abundance markets are here, they are real, and business leaders are starting to change the competitive landscape by lowering costs, increasing personalization, and unlocking new large-scale opportunities. As we've shown, the key here is to use the new machine, fueled by data and wrapped in a new commercial model, to lower costs dramatically. This opens the floodgates for massive scale.

Many digital naysayers overlook the overall potential for growth based on abundance markets. The more we work with customers and observe the market, the more confident we are that the doomsday prophets are as wrong today as they ever were.

Automation, Code Halos, enhancement, and abundance are all value levers for work that many companies are already practicing today. But what about the truly fresh idea? How can companies configure themselves to be ready to create the next Uber, Predix, Palantir, or x.ai? Balancing investment and nurturing new ideas for the future with running the business is always a tricky challenge. Many of us have grown up with the mythology of the lone inventor toiling away, crafting the Next Big Thing. It turns out, though, that there is both an art and a science to innovation. In the digital economy, we call this "discovery."

11 | Discovery

Manage Innovation for the Digital Economy

As we have seen throughout this book, the future of work will be fundamentally different when machines do everything. Discovering this future—through formal R&D processes *and* informal "ground-up" continuous improvement—is the focus of this last chapter dedicated to outlining our AHEAD model.

Discovery, aka blue-sky innovation, related to systems of intelligence and the digital economy, is both a catalyst for and an outcome of undertaking the preceding steps of AHEAD. Automating, instrumenting, enhancing, and making products and services abundant will all allow your organization to discover opportunities that were never before visible or addressable.

Discovery itself, though, is a philosophy, a rigorous practice, an openness to the future, an understanding that innovation can't be a side project—that is, something "nice-to-have" or a rounding error of spend buried deep in a 10-Q report. Discovery is central to remaining relevant in the great digital build-out that lies before us. While machines will do more and more of our current work, the process of innovation will allow us to discover entirely new things to do (with and without machines) that are impossible to imagine and hard to predict, but they will be at the core of what *we* do in the future.

We've touched on a number of historical figures throughout this book: Henry Ford, Thomas Edison, Ned Ludd, and many others. We start this chapter by looking at another far less well-known one: an inventor whose humble technological breakthrough 186 years ago has had an outsized impact across the world (particularly on Sunday afternoons at 4:00 PM), the evolution of which has something to teach us not only about how innovation works but how we can and should have faith that the unknown future will produce amazing opportunities.

Think for a moment about today's global sports industry, now worth up to $620 billion a year.[1] Factor in ancillary revenues (hot dogs sold at games, taxi and subway rides to sports arenas, ibuprofen taken after your team gets knocked out in the first round of the playoffs), and the total amount of money sports generates is probably way north of that figure.

All that spending flows, initially, from an English engineer's 1827 invention, the *lawn mower*. Edwin Budding came up with the idea for a small, hand-pushed machine as an alternative to the scythe—the traditional backbreaking way of cutting grass—after seeing how a blade in a cylinder was used in a local cloth mill.

To be sure, sports existed well before the lawn mower: Thomas Lord of Lord's Cricket Ground[2] fame was playing professional cricket in the late 18th century, and, don't forget, Jane Austen was writing about baseball in 1797.[3] But there was no "sports industry" as such. Clearing spaces to play cricket with a scythe was difficult, and thus they were few and far between; early types of footballs were kicked around on mainly muddy thoroughfares.

Budding's lawn mower, as shown in Figure 11.1, allowed grass to be cut easily and uniformly, and what had historically been simply fields of uncut long grass became a newly defined space: a "playing field." Over the subsequent decades, into the previously unthought-of vacuum of that open space, rushed idea after idea about things that could be done there. Very quickly an explosion of sporting innovation occurred: football/soccer (the Football Association formed in 1863), rugby (the Rugby Football Union formed in 1871), tennis (the Wimbledon Championship was first played in 1877), croquet (the first all-comers' meeting was in 1868). All these sports emerged to take place on the grass playing field.

Figure 11.1   Mr. Budding and the First Lawn Mower

Everything that we sports fans live and breathe stems from that original foundational innovation that created that "space."

If Edwin Budding could come back now and see the impact his lawn mower has had on the world, he would, no doubt, be astonished. It's unlikely that he could have imagined when he sold his first machine to Regent's Park Zoological Garden that 138 years later, a young professional footballer named Cristiano Ronaldo would have 200 million social media followers, all because he kicks a smallish ball around on a field of cut grass.[4]

Ronaldo's fame and all of the jobs and money associated with sports across the world originate from Budding's machine. The lawn mower is the foundation upon which the sports industry is built.

Systems of intelligence are the latest set of technologies creating foundations on which new industries and new jobs are being and will be built. Jobs of the future that today we simply can't imagine—just as Budding wouldn't have been able to extrapolate from his machine the rise of Ronaldo, or the commentator who talks about Ronaldo, or the equipment manufacturer that supplies Ronaldo, or the designer who created his logo. What one might call the *Budding Effect*.

Today, a new economy is emerging with a raft of job categories that even a few years ago would have been hard to predict: social-media consultants, search-engine optimizers, full-stack engineers, Perl developers, digital prophets, hackers-in-residence, content curators, chief happiness officers, innovation sherpas, clue shredders, pixel czars, chief ninjas. These are all jobs that the tech economy's equivalent to Edwin Budding (Babbage, Flowers, Turing, Noyce, Hopper, Gates, Andreessen, and Zuckerberg?) could not have imagined.

Though the notion of "build it and they will come" was largely discredited in the dot-com bust of the early 2000s, faith that the future *will* produce opportunity is paramount to any company or anyone navigating uncertain times. Otherwise, you might as well just keep on trying to take cost out of your old machines, your old business models, the old S-curves.

Therefore, the question you and your teams should be asking is: What are our lawn mowers? We're already seeing digital leaders place discovery bets on what their lawn mowers might be.

Mark Zuckerberg paid $2 billion for Oculus VR (developer of the Oculus Rift virtual-reality headset) in 2014, but acknowledged that the acquisition's focus on gaming was just a start:

> *Virtual reality was once the dream of science fiction. But the internet was also once a dream, and so were computers and smartphones. The future is coming, and we have a chance to build it together. I can't wait to start working with the whole team at Oculus to bring this future to the world, and to unlock new worlds for all of us.*[5]

AI is changing our world already, but in reality we've only begun to scratch the surface of where it will take us over the next 20, 50, or 100 years. As Robert High, the chief technology officer of IBM Watson, told us:

> *Our work on cognitive computing—about amplifying human cognition—is at a very early stage. I don't want it [the AI technology] to be as good as a human; I want it to be better. Economic value is going to drive the progression and evolution of these cognitive systems to a form of intelligence that I don't think we would recognize as being similar to human intelligence. It's not going to be a replication of human intelligence. It's going to be a replication of some small portion of human intelligence, and then a whole bunch of other forms of intelligence that we don't necessarily recognize today but which will be more beneficial economically. Think about astronomers and how much more they've learned by being able to create sensors in the infrared range, or the X-ray range, or ranges of the spectrum that humans aren't able to perceive. It wasn't necessary for humans to perceive it, wasn't necessary for human evolution or even survival. But it is extremely useful for understanding how the universe works.*

Your job is to imagine the new forms of value you can create with the new machines of the new revolution. AI may be a strange lawn mower (one, we hope, not related to Stephen King's *The Lawnmower Man*), but we trust you get the point. The Budding Effect has played out time after time throughout history, and it is playing out again now. Institutionalizing the role and importance of being open to the fruits of innovation is a hugely important role that you, as a leader of the future, even though you may not be the head of your company's formal R&D department, need to play.

In a world of cloud services, of open APIs, platforms, and crowdsourcing, every organization has access to readily affordable tools (that a short time ago were prohibitively expensive) with which to build the future of their work. The leaders, individual and corporate, in the digital build-out will be those who leverage the new "means of production"—those who break away from business as usual and choose to develop "business unusual." This is how you do that.

R&D Without AI Is No R&D at All

Soon, the new machine will be your platform of innovation. Once you are instrumenting, automating, tracking, and analyzing the core operations of your business and applying machine learning, innovation opportunities will be consistently unearthed. These will not be based on the informed opinions of individuals, whether executives or R&D staff, but rather on empiricism, on what's actually occurring in the business.

Now, "innovation" is a rich term, with many different attributes and applications. But the new machine can be applied to your R&D in numerous areas, including the following:

- Products and services
- Processes
- Business models
- Sustainability
- Frugality
- Experience
- Customer-led efforts
- Ecosystem/supply chain

With product innovation, for example, your team will gain continual insight as to how your products are (and aren't) being used, as to what customer frustration points exist, and where the obvious areas for improvement (both incremental and fundamental) exist.

The idea of performing R&D-based innovation without an AI platform will soon be viewed as nothing short of guessing. People in your company will look at the traditional centralized R&D group within corporate and begin to ask, "Who are those strange wizards?" We will eventually wonder, "How did we think having a few smart people in a room at corporate headquarters would deliver constant innovation?" It will seem . . . silly.

Why? How can a small group of people in one location compete with the insight and the learning of the AI platforms we've described in previous chapters? Once you have automated, haloed, and enhanced your company's activities, the associated AI engines can be applied to innovation. Your R&D process and current R&D team will be greatly enhanced by the application of the new machine, primarily because it radically accelerates the scale and speed of the innovation process.

Innovation at the Velocity and Scale of AI

As Netflix continues to grow, it is attempting, essentially, to create something entirely new—the world's first global television station. But this raises many significant challenges in developing content that will appeal to a wide variety of international customers. After all, it's difficult enough for a local television station to understand the preferences of viewers in a specific metropolitan area; such a station's programming managers live in that very community, with their fingers continuously on the pulse of its culture, demographics, preferences, and sensibilities. How could Netflix's team, based in Northern California, possibly understand the nuanced viewing preferences of customers in places like Bavaria, Australia's Northern Territory, or Japan's Okinawa Island? With the aid of the new machine, it's actually quite easy.

Netflix's programming managers deploy their algorithms to inform them about what is (and isn't) working with specific customer demographics around the globe. In fact, they are constantly surprised, finding their personal assumptions are usually quite wrong. Upon launching into Europe, for example, the Netflix team presumed that age was the key determinant of what customers would watch. Wrong.

Todd Yellin, head of product innovation at Netflix, said, "We thought the 19-year-old guy and the 70-year-old woman have such different tastes that personalization would be easy. But the truth is, 19-year-old guys like to watch documentaries about wedding dresses. Hitting play just once on the Netflix service, that's a far more powerful signal than your age and gender."[6] Similarly, geography doesn't matter as much as the Netflix team originally expected. Common sense told them that specific regions of the world would have very particular tastes. Wrong again. For example, many Japanese anime films are consumed outside of Japan. Concluded Yellin, "Now we have one big global algorithm, which is super helpful because it leverages all the tastes of all consumers around the world."

Had Netflix pursued a more traditional approach to R&D to understand global customer preferences (i.e., talking to studio heads, hiring high-priced consultants around the world, taking action based on the informed opinions of its most experienced staff), it likely would have made some very expensive mistakes. After some global failures, Netflix executives might have concluded, "Our model just doesn't work over there." Instead, by continually leveraging the insights generated by the new machine, the company benefits from a highly detailed roadmap for its ongoing expansion.

Innovation fueled by a system of intelligence is also fast. This rapid-fire, machine-based learning sits at the core of inventor and futurist Ray Kurzweil's Law of Accelerating Returns. In short, Kurzweil argues that humans learn at a linear rate, while machines now learn at an exponential pace. As such, when the new machine is soon widely adopted, the rate of human progress in the 21st century (as defined by the cumulative growth of human knowledge and the pace of innovation) will be at least 1,000 times the average rate of the 20th century.[7]

Now, will this thousand-fold speed improvement actually come to fruition? Probably not; there are many carbon-based factors that slow down innovation (e.g., people's opinions, ideas, and emotions, as well as many of the organizational inertial issues we've previously highlighted). So let's be conservative and bring Kurzweil's prediction down not just a bit, but a lot. Even if we lower the machine-based innovation rate by two orders of magnitude, that still means your R&D process will move at 10 times its current rate. This is a level of scale and speed that traditional R&D simply could never provide.

Is Blockchain Our Digital Lawn Mower?

Every few years in the tech industry, a technology of great promise comes along. Sometimes that promise is fulfilled (e.g., the Internet, smart-phones, social platforms). Sometimes it's not (e.g., Second Life, gami-fication, Google Glass).

If there were a specific technology that would win the current "buzz and hype" award, it is Blockchain—the distributed ledger in the sky that has the potential to automate not just key processes but also entire industries.

Goldman Sachs has said that Blockchain has "the potential to redefine transactions" and to change "everything."[8] Many voices are now predicting that it will fundamentally alter not just our banking system but other vital portions of the economy, such as document storage and management, contract management, and identity management.

Blockchain advocates believe it has the potential to automate the most basic functions of the banking system: lending, payments, and settlements. Consider all the settlements required each day by credit card transactions, stock trades, currency trades, loan origination, insurance settlements, and so forth. In the renowned catchphrase of Carl Sagan, "billions and billions."[9] And consider the vital societal role that banks, investment banks, credit-card companies, and insurance firms play to ensure that all of these settlements are managed transparently and securely. What if all of those settlements could be automated and in the process managed far faster, more cheaply, and more securely? Enter Blockchain, perhaps one of tomorrow's most potent technologies and a fertile direction for discovery.

And the potential use cases don't stop with financial services. For example, what if warranty management were handled not by centralized companies full of humans but was automated in the cloud by Blockchain? Say, for example, any instrumented machine that had encountered mechanical troubles (e.g., an air conditioner, a bus, a power generator) wouldn't have to wait for a series of humans to discover, diagnose, and then fix the problem. Instead, the machine would recognize the prob-lem, determine how it should be fixed, review its own warranty, summon the appropriate mechanic, manage the payment, and update all the appropriate records. All of this would be automated—with trust and efficiency—by Blockchain.

Blockchain pessimists, on the other hand, have a very simple argument: "Where's the beef?" They will note that industry use cases with Blockchain automating core processes of major corporations are still few and far between.

How, then, should we think about Blockchain? How do you manage through the confusion and take the appropriate actions in your company? We suggest you follow two parallel approaches, which can be applied to many new technologies and ideas.

- **Approach Blockchain like a call option.** Blockchain is like a risky, high-beta stock. It could go bust, or it could provide massive returns. Approach it as such. Make some small investments that could pay off handsomely if Blockchain takes off but small enough that you could walk away if Blockchain fizzles. To do this, ensure that several members of your core technology teams are immersed in all things Blockchain. Create alliances with key Blockchain technology vendors (both product and service). Launch a few small pilots in your company. Keep a close eye on use cases in other companies. See if it all makes sense.
- **Don't let the Blockchain tail wag the business dog.** As with all technology fads, there will be Blockchain fanatics in your midst. They will see Blockchain's applicability to almost *everything* in your company. We have seen several cases in which this thinking gained too much momentum inside a company, leading to false starts. In such instances, precious time, money, and effort are spent on technology-first initiatives without anybody asking "What's the business benefit here?"

One of the core principles of this book is that machines can do many things but that practical application should be focused on specific business processes and customer experiences. When you are making discovery investments, start at the process-and-experience level and imagine how the process can be restructured and reinvented with digital. Getting this backward and letting Blockchain or any other new technology (e.g., quantum computing, augmented reality, nuclear fusion) attract outsized investment can be a prescription for failure.

Discovery Is Hard, but Not as Hard as Being Irrelevant

If you need further ammunition to argue the importance of being open to discovery, the views of the world's largest investor, Larry Fink, may be useful. Fink, whose firm, BlackRock, Inc., has $4.6 trillion under management, is not the sort of guy you'd expect to be interested in anything other than next quarter's results. Yet Fink recently sent a letter to the CEOs of S&P 500 companies and large European corporations, stating, "We are asking that every CEO lay out for shareholders each year a strategic framework for long-term value creation. . . . Today's culture of quarterly earnings hysteria is totally contrary to the long-term approach we need."[10]

Fink's letter says, in essence, that companies need to recognize that an overemphasis on optimizing old approaches without giving enough priority to new approaches is having deleterious effects; indeed, the letter goes on to say "companies have not sufficiently educated [their shareholders] about . . . how technology and other innovations are impacting their business."

This type of insight is important in every organization that is trying to invent the future of their work. Living with failure is a prerequisite of creating long-term value. In his field guide to the start-up world of California, *Chaos Monkeys: Obscene Fortune and Random Failure in Silicon Valley*, former Facebook product manager Antonio Garcia-Martinez expresses the view that 90% of the 75% of companies that don't achieve "escape velocity" fail to do so because they simply give up; start-up life is *so* tough.

Discovery *is* a hard, unforgiving place to pitch a tent. There are no guarantees. Living with failure is contrary to so many personal and corporate instincts. Yet without this attitude—*this resilience*—your future probably looks an awful lot like your present, a present that is certainly soon to be your past. And that's not a future at all.

What to Do on Monday? Don't Short Human Imagination

Discovery can be a risk. Invest too much in the wrong ideas, and you go broke. Wait for somebody else to do it, and you can miss the market opportunity of a lifetime. Countless books have already been written about innovation methods, grandiose plans, and the future of society. Our goal here, however, is to give some practical advice wrapped in a single bold strategy.

That is, don't short human imagination. Succeeding in an era in which machines do almost everything also means accepting and believing that humans will have plenty to do.

If, as some techno-dystopians believe, machines will render humans irrelevant in the near future, the fundamental DNA of *Homo sapiens* that has propelled us forward for millennia will have run dry. What is that DNA attribute? It is *curiosity*, something that is the key defining characteristic of intelligence (as it is currently manifested in our human form). From our first words to our first steps, to our first journey, it is intrinsic to our very being to want to know who, what, why, and where. Nobody tells us to ask questions. No parent, or teacher, or TV show, or social media feed tells us or programs us to want to know what's up. We just do.

When computers start asking questions like "Just what do you think you're doing, Dave?," then we should start worrying. But that eventuality is as far off in the future as it was 50 years ago, when the first prophets of AI-induced human calamity became vocal. Until then, humans will continue to ask questions, be curious, imagine, and build, all the while *using* the new machine.

The trick is figuring out how to identify and nurture the next big (or small) idea, while balancing this against the reality of how investments are made in large and medium-sized companies. In fact, whenever we bring up discovery with clients, their first reflex is to assert, "But we don't have any money!"

With that in mind, the following subsections describe some things you can do to help balance the budget while still benefiting from the results of wisely conducted discovery.

Apply Digital Kaizen

So what's the best practice for bringing about this new form of innovation? We find too many managers looking for "the next great breakthrough" or, in baseball terms, the grand slam. That doesn't work.

The opposite approach is to ask how the new machine adds the most value—that is, by looking for continuous, incremental improvements or looking to hit singles on a consistent basis. This is akin to the Japanese concept of *kaizen*, which translates as "change for better" but is implemented as small, continuous improvements that in time have a large impact.

Through digital Kaizen—leveraging the new machine to be on the lookout for incremental improvements—the R&D function can be revolutionized. For example:

- In product innovation, AI platforms can help monitor a fleet of machines, enabling fast recognition of which components fail prematurely and why. This would then inform the next generation of engineering, as well as field service operations.
- With process innovation, AI will monitor an instrumented workflow and quickly recognize existing bottlenecks and recommend new approaches.
- With customer-led innovation, ongoing reviews of how customers are actually using your products will inform product management and pricing schemes.

These are the areas where the new machine can best be initially focused in R&D. They are clear examples of digital Kaizen, a series of small discoveries that over time can change the basis of competition.

For example, nothing is more important to colleges and universities than students—in particular, keeping them as students. The University of Kentucky (in Lexington) is dealing with retention in real-time by applying a bit of digital Kaizen. The school has employed a real-time data analytics platform and a team of data scientists to develop a predictive scoring system that provides here-and-now insight into individual student engagement levels. Data is collected by asking students short survey questions when they log into the school portal, perhaps whether they've purchased all their textbooks or to rate their stress level on a scale of 1 to 5. In just five weeks, the school collected data from more than 40,000 individual students. The insights gained helped increase freshman-to-sophomore retention by 1.3%—an apparently incremental improvement with a significant downstream impact.[11]

The best part: with a breakthrough innovation, your competitors will quickly look to neutralize it in the market. But with digital Kaizen, your moves are stealthy and thus difficult to replicate.

It's easy to get a case of whiplash when making realistic plans for discovery. By their very nature, specific ROIs and well-intended Gantt charts tend to inspire frustration when applied to discovery. The best partial antidote is to balance near-term realistic innovation—digital Kaizen, or perhaps "little d" discovery—with your own lawn mower or moon shot idea—"Big D" Discovery.

Digital Kaizen focuses on incremental moves for meaningful impact, a near-term project for which you can take responsibility. The path should be clear by now: cut costs with automation, instrument everything, and harvest the data "exhaust."

Your digital moon shot might be a project based on Blockchain, or quantum computing, or even artificial super-intelligence. These are bigger bets that, if you're thinking like a VC, can be taken in small steps over time.

The trick here is to balance both approaches.

Let Hits Pay for Misses

Another of the key principles of discovery is the notion best encapsulated by the scriptwriter William Goldman in his 1983 book about the film industry, *Adventures in the Screen Trade:* "nobody knows anything."

Your goal should be to become a Know-It-All business via instrumentation, sensors, big data, and analytics. However, the inherent unpredictability of the future is likely a permanent truth. Nobody really *knows* what will work on the road ahead; not even Netflix. Goldman says that people, if they're lucky, make "educated guesses." Code Halos can help educate us to make better guesses while making ignorance less acceptable, but we should be humble enough to know that we can't *really* know. This is particularly true in the wide open spaces now being created by our new lawn mowers.

To deal with this reality, you need to take a leaf out of Hollywood's book and structure your discovery-related efforts around the core idea that "hits pay for misses." Estimates suggest that 70% of movies lose money.[12] (Only estimates exist because movie industry accounting is surrounded by a long-standing *omertá*.) Similar ratios exist in other creative industries, such as music, books, and theater. Even the most revered actors or novelists have plenty of turkeys on their résumés. It's unlikely that Robert DeNiro's 2011 bomb, *New Year's Eve*, will feature heavily on the sad day *The New York Times* runs his obituary.

Of course the tech industry is full of its own misses: Microsoft's Vista, Facebook's phone, Apple's Lisa; even the mighty stumble a lot of the time.

Shikhar Ghosh of Harvard Business School believes 75% of venture-backed firms in the United States don't return their investors' capital.[13] Technology funding, both in the VC world and inside large companies, is expressly set up so that 70% (and higher) failure rates can be tolerated.

In thinking like a VC, recognize that success is determined by active portfolio management. It's not about putting all of one's money on one idea but making lots of investments, many of which actually don't pan out. According to data from a prominent investment firm, "Around half of all investments returned less than the original investment."[14] The analysis also notes that a paltry "6% of deals . . . made up 60% of total returns."

This may be sobering info. You may ask, "How can we get returns when the smart money does so poorly?" Well, you can move those odds in your favor, but the key is managing a portfolio, not avoiding failure. In fact, in the study cited, a fund gets better returns not by having fewer failures but by having more really big hits. In other words, they had to take more risks to get the best returns.

It turns out the best VCs (those with the highest and most consistent returns) achieve their success not just through superior management of their individual start-ups (i.e., finding great entrepreneurs with fantastic ideas and providing them with the right funding and support). More important, as evidenced by the data, is the simple fact that they place more bets and are willing to fail more often.

Even if you're not in a formal R&D role related to discovery, this means you should establish a portfolio of initiatives focused on discovery, with a clear life cycle methodology that manages these initiatives from inception through to ultimate success or failure. Some companies have initiated groups of entrepreneurially minded employees and allowed them to propose ideas for new products or services, secure financing and management support, build out a team to establish the ideas as a going concern in the external marketplace, and then attempt to grow it to a mature enough point that it can "graduate" to become part of the revenue-driving engine of the overall company. This helps balance digital Kaizen—discovering process-level innovation—with more blue-sky discovery: that is, seeking the next big hit. Toyota is doing just this—balancing investment in its traditional models while simultaneously working on driverless cars.

The Road to Driverless Cars

One of the places in which we've become totally reliant and comfortable with automation over the years has been in our cars. Manual (stick-shift) transmissions represent less than 4% of automobile sales in the United States.[15] Without us really noticing, our cars have become full of automation technology: windows, steering, cruise control, GPS, adaptive headlights—the list goes on. Automation has snuck up all around us to improve the driving experience.

The accelerated race to automation has now led us to the next frontier: the fully autonomous, self-driving car. Long a standard feature of sci-fi entertainment, from *Logan's Run* (1976) to the *Knight Rider* TV show (1982–1986) to *Total Recall* (1990) to *Minority Report* (2002), the self-driving car is fast (and furiously) becoming a reality.

Following Google's 2010 announcement that it was developing autonomous vehicles, major car manufacturers have buckled up and put the pedal to the metal to try to win this new race.[16] Ford, General Motors, Audi, Mercedes-Benz, and BMW, among others, are all in the process of introducing different flavors of autonomy into their fleets; some will be fully self-driving—most eye-catchingly, Ford's "no steering wheel/no pedal" model developed in conjunction with Google—while others, such as Audi's, will have a "highway traffic jam pilot" feature available by 2018. Famously, industry upstart Tesla has a "look Ma, no-hands" option already being (mostly) successfully driven by thousands of people.

Toyota—the world's number-one auto maker by sales, with more than 10 million vehicles sold in 2015—is increasing its investments in autonomy by spending $1 billion over the next five years on embedding sensors and AI into its cars.[17,18] The aim is to have a car that can drive itself on highways by the 2020 Tokyo Olympics.[19]

As Ned Curic, EVP of Technology and Development at Toyota Connected in Los Angeles, told us, "The business model is going to change, for sure. The way we actually sell vehicles will change in the next 10 years, and the way you deliver the mobility services will change. AI is going to play a huge role in the future. AI is the central technology that will change the experience."

And yet, amid these wrenching industry shifts, Curic said the future is uncertain: "If you believe Silicon Valley, nobody will be driving vehicles in 10 years. But the reality, at least, is showing something that is the opposite. We did research, and to our surprise, millennials do want to have a car and do want to drive. So we, as a company, have to hedge."

A fully autonomous vehicle may be Toyota's moon shot, but the company is also simultaneously working to make more modest, but still important, discoveries related to assisted driving.

Toyota sees a medium-term future in which autonomous cars are one option it sells within an overall range of cars for which higher levels of general automation become the norm but stop short of full automation. The fully self-driving car will appeal to a certain demographic, and for certain situations: elderly or disabled people will likely want them, and organizations operating in hazardous environments (such as a mine or an airport) will find them useful. Curic said he believes "you'll be able to drive a self-driving car within 10 years, without the driver needing to pay attention on many roads in America, but not on any road."

The important discovery lesson here is the notion of "hedging." Organizations trying to discover the future need to act like venture capitalists or movie studios, placing lots of bets rather than just one big bet. Nobody *really* knows with certainty how big the market for self-driving cars will be in 5, 10, or 20 years, but Toyota's leaders do know that if they don't invest here, they run the risk of losing a leadership position.

In addition to this approach being run across your company, you can also scale it down to the portfolio of things that you are directly responsible for in whatever part of the business you operate. If you run a finance function, actively seek ideas from your team on how to reduce month-end book-closing cycles; if you get 10 ideas, one or two of them might be worth exploring further. If you run a sales function, ask for recommendations for new tools that can increase conversion rates. Again, most of the suggestions will likely go nowhere, but semi-formalizing a culture that encourages seeking out new ideas is a powerful way of signaling that business as usual isn't the only business you're in.

Leave the Past Behind

Through our work with clients, we repeatedly hear variations on this lament: "We love your ideas. We'd love to build Code Halos and introduce systems of intelligence. We know we have to migrate to our digital future. *But* . . . We have such ingrained, complex, mission-critical systems that we can't change; we dare not risk cutting 'Wire X' because we simply don't know what will happen if we do."

Discovery initiatives in *many* Fortune 500 companies are hampered because of their expensive, sunk-cost, legacy technology. In an era when the competitive advantages of technology have never been greater, these organizations are maintaining (at huge expense) systems that are a terrible competitive *disadvantage*.

The reason for this is they don't have the ability to turn old stuff off.

Anyone who's been around corporate IT for a while knows that the concept of decommissioning systems (i.e., sunsetting them, killing them, *turning them off*) is entirely alien. Even when new systems, apps, and processes are developed, these typically "sit" on top of their predecessors. Systems are built on top of systems, and before you know it, you have a logical architecture that is the proverbial plate of spaghetti.

There has never been a culture in enterprise IT of throwing things away when they're past their sell-by date. No brownie points accrue to those who question the value of old systems or choose to wade into the often complicated and uncomfortable (potentially career-limiting) political issues around such matters: "Fred commissioned that app. I don't want to tell him, an executive VP, that the system's no good anymore."

On occasion, finance executives have tried to introduce ideas like "zero-based budgeting" to get IT to take a cold, hard look at the existing footprint but to little avail. Y2K proved that old systems never die. What little glory there is in IT comes from building new stuff, not dealing with old systems.

There are psychological dynamics in play as well, above and beyond spreadsheet dynamics. After all, shutting down old systems can feel like throwing away money. The Japanese writer Marie Kondo, whose book *The Life-Changing Magic of Tidying Up* has turned into an unlikely sales phenomenon (4.5 million copies sold and counting), says that the money you spent on the item was the price of the joy it generated while you used it.[20] If the item no longer "sparks joy," there is no need to hang onto it.

In accounting-speak, we might say the item is "fully depreciated." And *a lot* of IT is "fully depreciated," hardly generating any "joy" at all.

This is a problem. Without clearing away systems and processes that are no longer fit for purpose or soon won't be, organizations are undermining their ability to find the budget, time, resources, and *energy* to invest in the future. Given that most IT budgets increase by small margins year after year, it's unlikely that maintaining business as usual will lead companies to prioritize building and leveraging new machines.

Turning off old IT is difficult, of course, but strategies to deal with this conundrum *do* exist. Given the mission-critical nature of many IT systems, caution understandably must rule. No one would be too happy if American Airlines made mistakes with flight management software while we were at 35,000 feet. However, the reality is that unless IT (and business) executives get honest about the need to turn apps, systems, and processes *off*, they (and the companies they serve) are going to simply sit and watch the incredible opportunities of this new golden age slip further and further away.

As we move away from systems of record to systems of intelligence, the time is right again to consider which elements of the past will be useful in the future. As we illustrated in Chapter 4, systems of record *do* have a place in the new machines that you need to build, but not in their entirety, not all of them, and not as they are currently configured. Before you take another step forward, examine—or reexamine—your current IT and process port-folio with a steely eye. Chances are good you'll need to retain outside experts to give you the unvarnished truth. Most important, recognize that the cycles of technological innovation that we've examined throughout this book are moving so fast that it is entirely illogical to imagine that systems built 10, 20, or 30 years ago will withstand the competitive onslaught from systems built with the latest tools, techniques, and raw materials.

Play the Wayback Game

If you think discovery is something that's theoretically desirable but practi-cally impossible, it's time to reconsider. They say a picture is worth 1,000 words, so here's a 90-second exercise that helps prove the point.

Open a browser and check out the Internet Archive Wayback Machine (at https://archive.org/web/). As the name says, it's a nonprofit group with over 500 billion Web pages archived from the past decades. Then, just pick a company you know and check it out; poke around. Big companies including HP, Kodak, and IBM have loads of archived pages.

Initially, it's kind of fun in an "Oh, wow, do you remember *film*!?" way, but it's also fuel for a much deeper notion. The design and content of Kodak's website in 1997 is 20 years old, but it feels as dated as a wool bathing suit or penny-farthing bicycle. These sites were state-of-the-art in every way, but the world has changed miraculously since then. Those of us who were there at the time know we had no idea of what was to come. Humans simply have trouble extrapolating into the future. We're quite happy to be (rightfully) proud of our current moments. We believe we're at the zenith of development (technically, socially, etc.). We are hardwired to think of ourselves as being at the apex, but in reality we're just at the highest camp on the side of an infinitely high mountain. We simply can't envision how things could be in five or ten years.

One other lesson to learn from the Wayback Game is just how fast technology has changed. Many companies that ruled the day not too long ago—HP, CSC, EDS, Compaq, Gateway, Research in Motion, Nokia, etc.—are now either struggling or gone. If you are in the tech industry, this is business as usual, but as we've shown, digital is moving on to "work that matters." Banks, insurance companies, retailers, health care providers, and so forth must become used to a tech-sector velocity of change.

Create Your Own Budding Effect

Machines will do more and more, and the companies leading the change will thrive in a winner-take-most digital economy. Discovery shouldn't be passed on to your competitors or your successors. With the new machine, you have all the tools and resources for discovery. It's your challenge, and your opportunity.

Throughout the book, we've talked about great innovators like Watt, Ford, and Jobs, and we've also mentioned lesser ones like Edwin Budding. We believe that in the next 20 years there will be a whole new set of iconic innovators who transform their industries. We don't know who they are, where they are from, or what they will do. Nobody does.

However, with great confidence, we can predict that they will connect the Three M's and apply the principles of the AHEAD model to focus on the work that matters. Central to their generative acts will be the belief that something better can be created. The true core of discovery is, after all, hope.

12

Competing on Code

A Call to Action from the Future

In the three years that we've been developing this book, the debates about the pros and cons of AI have intensified, and the battle lines have become more and more firmly drawn.

In the one camp are the *utopians,* those who believe AI is set to usher in an age of miracles and wonder, of endless technological marvels and broad sunlit uplands. In the other camp are the *dystopians,* those who see a world of malevolent robots, evil overlords, and an underclass scratching a living in the ruins of the great American dream. Both camps have their high priests and evangelists; famed inventor and futurist Ray Kurzweil (cited in Chapter 11) sees 20,000 years of progress happening during the next 100 years.[1] The CEO of Allen Institute of Artificial Intelligence, Oren Etzioni, imagines a world in which people focus on "activities that are personally meaningful to them, like art."[2] Conversely, Tesla CEO Elon Musk calls AI "our greatest existential threat," and physicist Stephen Hawking prophesies that AI might be the last event in human history.[3]

Anyone paying attention to these debates can quickly feel bewildered by claim and counterclaim, as both camps make strong arguments. If AI does develop along its current trajectory, it isn't hard to imagine it leaving us behind in the not too distant future; then again, the future could be amazing—as long as *I'm inside the walled garden.*

AI for Pragmatists

The question you might ask as you approach the end of this book is: Which camp is right—utopian or dystopian?

The short answer? Neither.

The future won't be one extreme or the other; it won't be a utopia or a dystopia. We firmly believe, as we have argued throughout this book, that intelligent machines will increase living standards; create better, more satisfying jobs; allow us to solve big problems; and invent entirely new products, services, and experiences. But we also fully acknowledge the truth that intelligent machines will replace some occupations, put pressure on wages for many jobs, make some people's skills and capabilities irrelevant, and leave behind those unable to keep up and compete.

Between the extremes of the debate is the reality of what is going to happen in the next few years. Machines will learn to do more and more things; narrow AI will seep into every type of software, as well as an increasing range of physical products; systems of intelligence will expose the systems (and products, and processes, and organizations) that aren't intelligent; and customers will gravitate to the Google or Amazon price.

These things will happen—*there is no doubt*—while the AI debates continue to rage.

The debate has, so far, been in the hands of theoreticians. It's now time for pragmatists to take over, pragmatists who realize that the past has never been singularly utopian or dystopian. After all, the best-selling record in England in 1967, the year many musicologists believe was the greatest ever with the Beatles at the zenith of their fame, was Engelbert Humperdinck's "Release Me." The past has always contained both; therefore, pragmatists logically believe the future will contain both, as well.

Pragmatists know that the debates will never be settled and fully agreed upon; but they know that arguing over possible futures ahead is less meaningful than *making a probable* future AHEAD. Pragmatists will be responsible for navigating their companies through the coming years, which

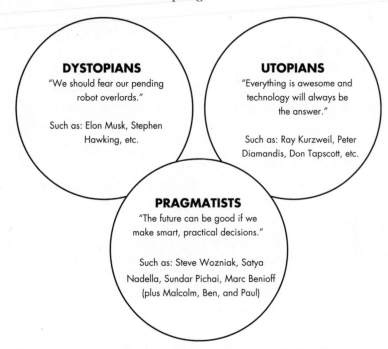

Figure 12.1   Utopians vs. Dystopians vs. Pragmatists

all of us—utopians and dystopians alike—can agree will be full of change, disruption, opportunity, and risk.

The Digital Build-Out Is Here

In this book, we have argued that the information-technology innovations and investments of the past 70 years are merely a precursor to the next waves of digitization, which will have truly revolutionary impacts on every aspect of work, society, and life. Just as the world of 1840s England was not unlike that of 1770s England but was utterly different from 1870s England (at the end of the *Second* Industrial Revolution), the compounding and exponential nature of digital progress is set to make the next 15 years a period of fundamental metamorphosis.

If you sometimes think the way you file an insurance claim today is pretty much the same as when you first did so back in 1973, or that a visit to the division of motor vehicles seems unchanged from when you first got your driver's license, you're right; technology has only brushed the edges of how these institutions work. But in 15 years' time, these experiences, along with a raft of others, will be entirely unrecognizable.

What will your company's products and services look like in 2030? Will they be smart, personalized, full of intelligence, and offered at price points that unlock huge new addressable markets? Or will they be only marginally better than they are today, run on systems built in the 20th century, with processes full of paper and duplication and work-arounds? Will they still stink?

The great digital build-out that is in front of us is going to see us double down on work that matters. The winning companies (and the executives who lead them) are going to improve and upgrade how we manage our money, our health, the physical infrastructure of our cities and towns, as well as how we equip our kids with what they need to succeed, how we conduct government, and how we secure ourselves against those who would do us harm. Systems of intelligence will be at the heart of all these efforts to make our society better.

Align the Three M's

As the last S-curve's growth rate continues its inexorable journey south (and our politicians argue over how its spoils are distributed), the new S-curve is gathering momentum, and so are the companies poised to lead this new charge. These are the companies that have learned how to master the Three M's: how to align the new raw materials of the digital age (data), the new machines (systems of intelligence), and the new models (business models that optimize the monetization of data-based personalization). These are the companies that understand how to build and operate a Know-It-All business, that understand that intelligent machines aren't to be feared but embraced and harnessed, and that are energized by the unwritten future rather than just trying to hang onto the glories of the past.

Even when machines can do everything, it will still be people who are the ultimate X factor. And certainly for the foreseeable future, it will be people like you who need to decide to instrument everything; to harvest all of the resulting data; to ask questions of the data; and to teach the learning algorithms what to look for, what is meaningful, and what is immaterial. It is people who need to make the decisions about investing in Hadoop, in BigML or Hive, in AWS or Oracle's cloud. It is people who need to do the hard work of deciding that a once-successful product is no longer worth keeping alive.

These difficult questions along with a million others are the ones you need to answer today while debates about what "intelligence" is stretch out into an infinite horizon. (As Wikipedia dryly notes, "the definition of intelligence is controversial."[4])

It is leaders like you who need to know what to do when machines do everything. It is for leaders like you that we have written this book.

Move AHEAD

Our AHEAD model is our recommendation for what you should do:

- Automate everything you can.
- Instrument everything you can.
- Enhance every person you can.
- Drive the price point of your products and services down as low as you can.
- Discover and invent all of the possible futures you can.

By automating, you strip the costs out of processes, speed processes up, improve process quality, and achieve "beyond-human" scale.

By instrumenting and creating a Code Halo, you turn everything into a "data generator," allowing you to see facts that have never been visible before.

By enhancing people and systems and processes through new technologies, you improve human performance levels. Multiply that by 1,000 or 100,000 people (or however many are in your organization), and in sum, you improve your corporate performance level.

By lowering the price of what you sell, you increase the size of the market you are serving; at an appropriate price point your offering has the potential to become abundant.

By prioritizing innovation, you increase your chances of discovering the future of your work.

The companies that are getting ahead are the ones acting on these ideas. Some companies we work with emphasize one "play" over another, while others recognize the holistic connection between all of the plays: automation enables enhancement, discovery uncovers how to achieve abundance, and so on.

All of them, however, understand the need to act now, to not wait for more certain times ahead, more clarity over exactly what AI is, and what it will become. All of them recognize that the rise of machine intelligence is the ultimate game changer we face today. All of them know that inaction will result in irrelevance. All of them know that fortune favors the brave and punishes the timid.

Courage and Faith in the Future

This is no time to be timid; just look at these quotes from recent news articles:

- "In 2014, for the first time, an e-sport's streamed broadcast attracted more viewers than the NBA Finals. More than 27 million people around the world tuned in to the League of Legends World Championship."[5]
- "General Motors is launching a car-sharing program. It's called Maven, it's available in exactly one city, and frankly, it's an unexciting riff on ZipCar. But GM isn't really competing with ZipCar. It's placing a bet on the future."[6]
- "'Speed is the new currency of business. The most dangerous place to make a decision is *in* the office,' says Salesforce.com CEO Marc Benioff."[7]
- "Digital Asset Holdings, the Blockchain start-up run by former JPMorgan Chase & Co. banker Blythe Masters, raised $52 million from investors and won a contract to radically speed up settlement in Australia's stock market."[8]
- "The [Sony] team's Flow Machines project successfully created . . . *Daddy's Car,* an AI-composed song that's meant to follow the musical style of The Beatles."[9]
- "What happened is the instantaneous and disembodied transfer of the photon's quantum state onto the remaining photon of the entangled pair, which is the one that remained six kilometres away at the university."[10]

What do all these quotes have in common? They are all messages from the future, telling us the world is changing faster than ever. Some of these you may not appreciate today, but in 10 years they could be part of our daily lives.

Approaches, norms, models, and ways of life that have been the backdrop during our 50 years (give or take!) on planet Earth and that one might have assumed would long outlast us are seemingly crumbling before our very eyes. Watching sports on TV, owning a car, answering a message the next day, planning to hold the same job for years, using a bank; all are going the way of all flesh.

This incredible pace of change, and the substantive nature of this change, is, at its core, about one thing: *what to do when machines do everything*.

Innovation shows no signs of stopping (despite our elevated perch on Maslow's Hierarchy of Needs) and shows no sign of being any less powerful than it has been in the past; quite the opposite.[11] Remember, *don't short human imagination*. The future is racing toward big businesses through the apps and Web services they use to get to the airport, hire new recruits, segment audiences, collaborate, meet, book hotels, ship goods, and access bandwidth and CPUs. All this abundance—functionality delivered at price points that are blowing away incumbent competition—is the light of innovation, of new ideas and approaches, of the *future*, that is there for everyone to see and follow and use.

The new frontiers we have explored in this book aren't simply about substituting labor with software; they're about building the new machines that will allow us to achieve higher levels of *human* performance. As Narrative Science's Kris Hammond—a pragmatist at heart—put it to us, "AI is not a mythical unicorn. It's the next level of productivity tool."

As we have seen throughout the preceding pages, innovation has propelled humans forward through the centuries; although the process of innovation is always messy and often uncomfortable (or worse), its power is entirely unstoppable.

Hammond, as one of the world's leading AI practitioners, sees the inevitability of widespread AI in the workplace: "I don't believe that work on AI can be inhibited. It's not like stem cells where there are physical things you can do to stop stem cell research. There is nothing physical you can do to stop AI research. The computational resources are out there."

As we have repeatedly illustrated, AI isn't coming; it's here. What this book attempts to do is show you there are things—many, many things—that you can do—*must do*—when machines do everything. Those who win in the coming great digital build-out, who seize the incredible rewards, who make history, will be those who stop debating and start building—and, rather than predicting the future, go out and invent it, hand-in-hand with the new machines.

Acknowledgments

Writing a book is really a community affair, and we would like to acknowledge the contribution of just a few of the many people who helped us along the way.

We are extremely grateful to the following visionaries and innovators who generously gave their time to speak with us as we developed the ideas represented in this book: Joseph Sirosh at Microsoft; Stuart Frankel and Kris Hammond at Narrative Science; Flavio Villanustre and David Glowacki at LexisNexis; Joel Rose at New Classrooms; Stephen Laster at McGraw-Hill Education; Ned Curic at Toyota; Max Yankelevich at Work Fusion; Jude Dieterman and Larry Bridge from TriZetto; Matt Wood at Amazon Web Services; Brett Tromp and Emile Stipp at Discovery Health; Robert High at IBM Watson; Dennis Mortensen at x.ai; Joe Procopio at Automated Insights; Xavier Peich at SmartHalo; and Anne Filson and Gary Rohrbacher from Filson-Rohrbacher.

In many cases we've built on research and insights from Cognizant's Center for the Future of Work, and we'd like to particularly thank Robert Brown, Manish Bahl, Euan Davis, Kevin Benedict, and the rest of the team for their work developing the ideas in this book.

We'd also like to thank the many Cognizant associates (too numerous to mention) who wake up every day intent on doing the best for clients. In particular, we'd like to thank Sowri Santhanakrishnan, Kaushik Bhaumik, Lee Saber, and Zacharyah Abend. Many others graciously added to their responsibilities by helping to connect us to their customers so we could learn more about what they are doing.

We'd also like to thank: Carlota Perez from the London School of Economics; Amanda Boxtel and Charles Engelbert; Clive Gravett from the Budding Foundation; Arielle Sobel from Betterment; J. P. Gownder from Forrester Research; Deia Campanelli, Mailee Garcia, and Amy Magee from General Electric Transportation; and Izabela Teixeira from GE Corporate.

Many thanks to Tara Owen, who helped us shape our thinking and language. Also to Todd Sattersten for helping us frame our initial concepts. Mary Brandel and Mark Baven worked tirelessly to improve and tighten the manuscript, collect data, and ensure we had all the right permissions in place. Alan Dino and Ian Koviak at The Book Designers helped us with the internal and external art. We'd like to also thank Ned Ward and the team at Stern Strategy Group for helping us get the word out. Thanks also to the team from Wiley for again helping us through the publishing process. We greatly appreciate the support of Roubini ThoughtLab, an independent research group overseen by renowned U.S. economist Nouriel Roubini. Lou Celi, Julien Beresford, and Daniel Miles helped us conduct our global study on how businesses can respond to the emerging digital economy.

We'd also like to recognize the following people who helped us coordinate the interviews we conducted: Jennifer Janzen, Helen Baric, Alice Robins, Jessica Lorti, Jennifer Kohn, Rebecca Owens-Martel, Glenda Misawa, Adam Devine, Robert Swinkin, Grant Milne, Emile Schachter, Loretta Fesler, Stefanie Syman, Gabrielle Gardner, Amy Ingram (even though "she" doesn't "exist"), and James Kotecki.

We'd especially like to thank Francisco D'Souza, CEO of Cognizant, who has continued to offer steadfast support as we've researched and written this book.

Finally, and most important, we'd like to thank our families for their seemingly endless patience, love, and encouragement throughout the years of putting this book together. Book authorship, on top of our work with business leaders around the world, demanded even more from our families. They kept us going, and kept the faith, throughout many (many) days and nights. It would take authors far more poetic than the three of us to fully express our gratitude to them.

Malcolm Frank, Paul Roehrig, Ben Pring
New York; Washington, D.C.; Boston, November 2016

Photo Credits

Page 6: Jon Stein, Betterment CEO & Founder | Source: Betterment

Page 15: Luddites | Source: Mary Evans Picture Library/Alamy Stock Photo

Page 22: Abstract of global communication | Pedro/Alamy Stock Photo

Page 30: New Classroom learning space | Source: New Classroom

Page 79: An assembly line of the Ford Motor Co. | Source: Chronicle/Alamy Stock Photo

Page 79: 1930s accounting department | Source: ClassicStock/Alamy Stock Photo

Page 101 (top): Airport check-in kiosks at Toronto Pearson International Airport | Source: Oleksiy Maksymenko/Alamy Stock Photo

Page 101 (middle): E-ZPass sign on the Pennsylvania Turnpike, United States | Source: JG Photography/Alamy Stock Photo

Page 101 (bottom): ATMs at Changi Airport | Source: Adrian Lim, Creative Commons, https://creativecommons.org/licenses/by/2.0/legalcode

Page 122: GE Transportation infographic | Source: GE Transportation

Page 140: McGraw-Hill Education's ALEKS classroom | Source: Kirk Tuck, photographer

Page 149: Sigourney Weaver, *Aliens,* 1986, directed by James Cameron | Source: ScreenProd/Photononstop/Alamy Stock Photo

Page 150: Amanda Boxtel with Elizabeth Pettit, Physical Therapist | Source: Charles Engelbert, photographer

Page 169: Reproduction of original patent drawing of Budding lawn mower, published 1830 alongside patent application | Source: The Budding Foundation

Disclaimers

Google, AlphaGo, Google Glass, DeepMind, Waze, Nest and YouTube are registered trademarks of Google, Inc.

Uber is a registered trademark of Uber Technologies, Inc.

Microsoft, PowerPoint, Cortana, Bing, Vista, and Excel are registered trademarks of Microsoft Corp.

Jeopardy! is a registered trademark of Jeopardy Productions, Inc.

Facebook is a registered trademark of Facebook, Inc.

iPhone, Mac, Apple Watch, iTunes, iPad, and Siri are registered trademarks of Apple, Inc.

Hadoop, Cassandra, and Hive are registered trademarks of The Apache Software Foundation!

BigML is a registered trademark of BigML, Inc.

Zipcar is a registered trademark of Zipcar, Inc.

Instagram is a registered trademark of Instagram, LLC

ALEKS is a registered trademark of ALEKS Corp.

McGraw-Hill Connect and McGraw-Hill LearnSmart are registered trademarks of McGraw-Hill Global Education Holdings LLC

Vitality is a registered trademark of Discovery Holdings Ltd.

Wikipedia is a registered trademark of the Wikimedia Foundation, Inc.

Dropbox is a registered trademark of Dropbox, Inc.

Airbnb is a registered trademark of Airbnb, Inc.

NIKE is a registered trademark of Nike, Inc.

Alexa Web Information Service, Amazon Web Services and Amazon S3 are registered trademarks of Amazon Web Services, Inc.

Amazon and Amazon Echo are registered trademarks of Amazon Technologies, Inc.

Ford and Mustang are registered trademarks of Ford Motor Co.

General Electric, GE, GoLINC, Trip Optimizer, LocoVision and Predix are registered trademarks of General Electric Co.

Strava is a trademark of Strava, Inc.

LinkedIn is a trademark of LinkedIn Corp.

LEGO is a trademark of The LEGO Group

LexisNexis and Lexis are registered trademarks of Reed Elsevier Properties, Inc.

Twilio is a registered trademark of Twilio, Inc.

Braintree is a registered trademark of PayPal, Inc.

SendGrid is a registered trademark of SendGrid, Inc.

Oracle, Peoplesoft, Java, and MySQL are registered trademarks of Oracle Corp.

Fitbit is a registered trademark of Fitbit, Inc.

IBM and IBM Watson are registered trademarks of IBM

Philips is a registered trademark of Koninklijke Philips N.V.

Under Armour is a registered trademark of Under Armour, Inc.

Toyota is a registered trademark of Toyota Motor Corp.

Yahoo! is a registered trademark of Yahoo! Inc.

ESPN is a trademark of ESPN, Inc.

Minor League Baseball is a registered trademark of Minor League Baseball

E-ZPass is a registered trademark of Port Authority of New York and New Jersey

AiCure is a registered trademark of AIC Innovations Group, Inc.

NextAngles is a registered trademark of MphasiS Ltd.

NVIDIA is a trademark of NVIDIA Corp.

Bvlgari is a registered trademark of Bulgari S.p.A.

Fendi is a registered trademark of Fendi Adele S.r.l.

Pink and Thomas Pink are registered trademarks of Thomas Pink, LLC

Oculus Rift is a registered trademark of Oculus VR, LLC

Betterment is a registered trademark of Betterment Holdings, Inc.

Artificial Intelligent Blockchain is a trademark of AI Coin, Inc.

Battlestar Galactica is a registered trademark of Universal City Studios, Inc.

Netflix is a registered trademark of Netflix, Inc.

Twitter is a registered trademark of Twitter, Inc.

Goldman Sachs is a registered trademark of Goldman, Sachs & Co.

Morgan Stanley is a registered trademark of Morgan Stanley

Credit Suisse is a registered trademark of Credit Suisse Group AG Société Anonyme (SA)

Cognizant and Code Halo are registered trademarks of Cognizant Technology Solutions U.S. Corporation

Cisco and Cisco Systems are registered trademarks of Cisco Systems, Inc.

Siemens is a registered trademark of Siemens Aktiengesellschaft

Progressive Auto Insurance is a trademark of Progressive Casualty Insurance Company

McKinsey is a registered trademark of McKinsey Holdings, Inc.

Oldsmobile, Buick, Chevrolet, Pontiac, Maven, GM, and Cadillac are registered trademarks of General Motors, LLC

New York Stock Exchange is a registered trademark of NYSE Group, Inc.

Oxford University is a registered trademark of The Chancellor Masters and Scholars of the University of Oxford

E*Trade is a registered trademark of E*TRADE Securities, Inc.

Merriam-Webster is a trademark of Merriam-Webster, Inc.

Lex Machina is a registered trademark of Lex Machina, Inc.

SalesForce is a trademark of salesforce.com, Inc.

SAP and SAP Hana are registered trademarks of SAP SE

Orange Is the New Black is a registered trademark of Lions Gate Entertainment, Inc.

TV Guide is a registered trademark of TV Guide Online Holdings, LLC

House of Cards is a trademark of MRC II Distribution Company, L.P.

Orphan Black is a trademark of Temple Street Releasing Limited

The Walking Dead is a trademark of Robert Kirkman, LLC

Akamai is a trademark of Akamai Technologies, Inc.

Limelight is a trademark of RightsFlow, Inc.

Level 3 Communications is a trademark of Level 3 Communications, LLC

Fitbit is a trademark of Fitbit, Inc.

Tesla is a trademark of Tesla Motors, Inc.

Walmart.com is a trademark of Wal-mart Stores, Inc.

Target is a trademark of Target Brands, Inc.

Macy's is a trademark of Macy's Department Stores

Sears is a trademark of Sears Brands, LLC

Honeycomb is a trademark of Roambee Corporation

Palantir is a trademark of Palantir Technologies, Inc.

Airbus and A350 are registered trademarks of Airbus SAS

Lidar Compressor is a registered trademark of Celartem, Inc., DBA Lizardtech

Bluetooth is a registered trademark of Bluetooth Sig, Inc.

Zigbee is a registered trademark of Zigbee Alliance Corporation

Bosch is a registered trademark of Robert Bosch GmbH

Samsung is a trademark of Samsung Electronics Co., Ltd.

First Data is a registered trademark of First Data Corporation

American Express is a registered trademark of American Express Marketing & Development Corp.

Boeing and 787 Dreamliner are registered trademarks of The Boeing Company

WeWork is a registered trademark of WeWork Companies, Inc.

SAS GO and SAS PLUS are registered trademarks of Scandinavian Airlines System Denmark-Norway-Sweden

McDonald's is a registered trademark of McDonald's Corporation

Holiday Inn is a registered trademark of Intercontinental Hotels Group

Toyota Connected is a trademark of Toyota Jidosha Kabushiki Kaisha TA Toyota Motor Corporation

Six Sigma is a trademark of Motorola Trademark Holdings LLC.

The Washington Post is a registered trademark of WP Company, LLC

USA Today is a registered trademark of Gannett Satellite Information Network, LLC.

Narrative Science is a registered trademark of Narrative Science, Inc.

Automated Insights is a registered trademark of Automated Insights, Inc.

The New York Times is a registered trademark of The New York Times Company

The Wall Street Journal is a registered trademark of Dow Jones, L.P.

Talla is a trademark of Talla, Inc.

Wired is a trademark of Advance Magazine Publishers, Inc.

TriZetto is a registered trademark of TriZetto Corporation

John Deere is a registered trademark of Deere & Company

Caterpillar is a registered trademark of Caterpillar, Inc.

Adidas is a registered trademark of Adidas AG joint stock company

BMW is a registered trademark of Bayerische Motoren Werke Aktiengesellschaft

Mercedes-Benz is a registered trademark of Daimler AG Corporation

Allstate is a registered trademark of Allstate Insurance Company

Travelers is a registered trademark of The Travelers Indemnity Company Corporation

BNSF Railway is a registered trademark of BNSF Railway Company

Sourcemap is a registered trademark of Sourcemap, Inc.

Pandora is a registered trademark of Pandora Media, Inc.

Reddit is a trademark of Reddit, Inc.

Mashable is a registered trademark of Mashable, Inc.

Tumblr is a registered trademark of Tumblr, Inc.

Hotel Tonight is a registered trademark of Hotel Tonight, Inc.

New Classrooms is a registered trademark of New Classrooms Innovation Partners

Anthem is a registered trademark of Anthem Insurance Companies, Inc.

Sony Pictures is a registered trademark of Sony Kabushiki Kaisha TA Sony Corporation

Ashley Madison is a registered trademark of Ruby Life, Inc.

Comcast is a trademark of Comcast Corporation

Iora Health is a registered trademark of Iora Health, Inc.

Da Vinci HD Surgical System is a registered trademark of Intuitive Surgical, Inc.

ImagineCare is a trademark of Mary Hitchcock Memorial Hospital nonprofit corporation

Prezi is a registered trademark of Prezi, Inc.

MIT is a registered trademark of Massachusetts Institute of Technology Corporation

WorkFusion is a registered trademark of Crowd Computing Systems, Inc.

Zappos.com and Zappos are registered trademarks of Zappos IP, Inc.

Pret A Manger is a registered trademark of Pret A Manger Limited

Starship Troopers is a registered trademark of TriStar Pictures, Inc.

Alien is a registered trademark of Twentieth Century Fox Film Corporation

Sarcos is a registered trademark of Raytheon Company

Ekso Bionics is a registered trademark of Ekso Bionics, Inc.

University of California is a registered trademark of The Regents of the University of California

In-Q-Tel is a registered trademark of In-Q-Tel, Inc.

Central Intelligence Agency is a trademark of Central Intelligence Agency

Spotify is a registered trademark of Spotify AB Corporation

Kodak is a registered trademark of Eastman Kodak Company

Blockbuster is a registered trademark of Blockbuster LLC

Nokia is a registered trademark of Nokia Corporation

Walgreens is a registered trademark of Walgreen Co.

Harvard Business School is a registered trademark of President and Fellows of Harvard College

Louis Vuitton is a registered trademark of Louis Vuitton Malletier

TAG Heuer is a registered trademark of LVMH Swiss Manufactures SA Corporation

HP and Hewlett Packard is a trademark of Hewlett-Packard Development Company, L.P.

Marriott is a registered trademark of Marriott International, Inc.

x.ai is a trademark of x.ai Corporation

Wimbledon is a registered trademark of All England Lawn Tennis Club (Wimbledon) Limited

Second Life is a registered trademark of Linden Research, Inc.

BlackRock is a registered trademark of BlackRock, Inc.

University of Kentucky is a registered trademark of University of Kentucky

Knight Rider is a registered trademark of Universal City Studios, LLC

Total Recall is a registered trademark of StudioCanal, S.A.

Minority Report is a registered trademark of Paramount Pictures Corporation

Audi is a registered trademark of AUDI AKTIENGESELLSCHAFT Corporation

American Airlines is a registered trademark of American Airlines, Inc.
Wayback Machine is a registered trademark of Internet Archive
CSC is a registered trademark of Computer Sciences Corporation
EDS is a registered trademark of Electronic Data Systems Corporation
Compaq is a registered trademark of Compaq Trademark B.V. Private, LLC
Research in Motion is a registered trademark of Research in Motion Limited
BigML is a registered trademark of BigML, Inc.
NBA and NBA the Finals are registered trademarks of NBA Properties, Inc.
Digital Asset Holdings is a trademark of Digital Asset Holdings, LLC
JPMorgan Chase is a registered trademark of JPMorgan Chase Bank, N.A.
The Beatles is a registered trademark of Apple Corps Limited

Notes

Chapter 1: When Machines Do Everything

1. Christopher Moyer, "How Google's AlphaGo Beat a Go World Champion," *The Atlantic*, March 28, 2016, http://www.theatlantic.com/technology/archive/2016/03/the-invisible-opponent/475611/.
2. "Automated Vehicle Crash Rate Comparison Using Naturalistic Data," January 8, 2016, http://www.vtti.vt.edu/featured/?p=422.
3. Emel Akan, "World's Top Hedge Fund Managers Took Home $13 Billion in 2015," *Epoch Times*, May 17, 2016, http://www.theepochtimes.com/n3/2067771-worlds-top-hedge-fund-managers-took-home-13-billion-in-2015/.
4. Todd Ackerman, "Houston invention: Artificial Intelligence to read mammograms" *San Antonio Express-News*, Sept. 16, 2016, http://www.expressnews.com/local/prognosis/article/Houston-researchers-develop-artificial-9226237.php.
5. Klaus Schwab, *The Fourth Industrial Revolution*, World Economic Forum, Jan. 11, 2016, https://www.amazon.com/Fourth-Industrial-Revolution-Klaus-Schwab-ebook/dp/B01AIT6SZ8.
6. John Kennedy, "Kara Swisher: 'In Silicon Valley, There Are a Lot of Big Minds Chasing Small Ideas,'" Silicon Republic, June 24, 2015, https://www.siliconrepublic.com/start-ups/kara-swisher-in-silicon-valley-there-are-a-lot-of-big-minds-chasing-small-ideas.
7. "Human Error Accounts for 90% of Road Accidents," *International News*, April 2011, http://www.alertdriving.com/home/fleet-alert-magazine/international/human-error-accounts-90-road-accidents.
8. See http://www.rmiia.org/auto/traffic_safety/Cost_of_crashes.asp and http://www.who.int/violence_injury_prevention/publications/road_

traffic/world_report/en/ and https://en.wikipedia.org/wiki/United_States_federal_budget.

9. http://www.fao.org/save-food/resources/keyfindings/en.

10. "Surprising Number of Emergency Room Medical Errors," July 15, 2016, http://philadelphia.cbslocal.com/2016/07/15/surprising-number-of-emergency-room-medical-errors/.

11. http://www.cbsnews.com/news/12-million-americans-misdiagnosed-each-year-study-says/ and http://www.healthcareitnews.com/news/deaths-by-medical-mistakes-hit-records.

12. http://www.cbsnews.com/news/us-education-spending-tops-global-list-study-shows/ and http://www.pewresearch.org/fact-tank/2015/02/02/u-s-students-improving-slowly-in-math-and-science-but-still-lagging-internationally/.

13. "Millennials hire computers to invest their money," *Denver Post*, March 4, 2016, http://www.denverpost.com/2016/03/04/millennials-hire-computers-to-invest-their-money/.

14. Julie Verhage, "Robo-Adviser Betterment Hits the $5 Billion Mark," *Bloomberg Markets*, July 14, 2016, http://www.bloomberg.com/news/articles/2016-07-14/robo-adviser-betterment-hits-the-5-billion-mark.

15. Melody Hahm, "Robo-advisor Wealthfront is now using AI to manage over $3 billion in assets," *Yahoo! Finance*, March 31, 2016, https://beta.finance.yahoo.com/news/robo-advisor-wealthfront-artificial-intelligence-betterment-assets-venmo-205354921.html and Michael P. Regan, "Robo Advisers to Run $2 Trillion by 2020 if This Model Is Right," Bloomberg, June 18, 2015, http://www.bloomberg.com/news/articles/2015-06-18/robo-advisers-to-run-2-trillion-by-2020-if-this-model-is-right.

16. For more information on Code Halos, see our white paper and book, https://www.cognizant.com/code-halos.

Chapter 2: From Stall to Boom: We've Been Here Before

1. "March of the Machines," *The Economist*, June 25, 2016, p. 11, http://www.economist.com/news/leaders/21701119-what-history-tells-us-about-future-artificial-intelligenceand-how-society-should.

2. Quoted in Klaus Schwab, *The Fourth Industrial Revolution*, January 2016, http://www3.weforum.org/docs/Media/KSC_4IR.pdf.

3. Carl Benedikt Frey and Michael Osborne, "The Future of Employment: How Susceptible Are Jobs to Computerisation?" Oxford Martin

Programme on Technology & Employment, Sept. 17, 2013, http://www.oxfordmartin.ox.ac.uk/downloads/academic/The_Future_of_Employment.pdf.

4. "Technology Isn't Working," *The Economist,* Oct. 4, 2014, http://www.economist.com/news/special-report/21621237-digital-revolution-has-yet-fulfil-its-promise-higher-productivity-and-better.

5. "United States GDP Growth Rate 1947-2016," Trading Economics, http://www.tradingeconomics.com/united-states/gdp-growth.

6. Carlota Perez, "The New Technological Revolution," Presentation at the Technology Frontiers Forum of *The Economist,* March 5, 2013, http://dev1.carlotaperez.org/.

7. Wikipedia entry on the motorcycle industry in China, https://en.wikipedia.org/wiki/Motorcycle_industry_in_China.

8. David Rose, *Enchanted Objects: Innovation, Design, and the Future of Technology* (New York: Scribner, 2015), https://www.amazon.com/Enchanted-Objects-Innovation-Design-Technology/dp/1476725640.

9. Dave Evans, "The Internet of Things: How the Next Evolution of the Internet Is Changing Everything," Cisco, April 2011, http://www.cisco.com/c/dam/en_us/about/ac79/docs/innov/IoT_IBSG_0411FINAL.pdf.

10. "A Guide to the Internet of Things," Intel Corp., http://www.intel.com/content/www/us/en/internet-of-things/infographics/guide-to-iot.html.

11. "IoT Market Forecast at $11 Trillion, Report Finds," *InformationWeek,* June 29, 2015, http://www.informationweek.com/strategic-cio/digital-business/iot-market-forecast-at-$11-trillion-report-finds/a/d-id/1321100.

12. "IDC Expects Global Wearable Device Shipments to Surge from 76.1 Million in 2015 to 173.4 Million Units by 2019," IDC, Sept. 14, 2015, http://www.idc.com/getdoc.jsp?containerId=prUS25903815.

13. Leo Sun, "Internet of Things in 2016: 6 Stats Everyone Should Know," The Motley Fool, Jan. 18, 2016, http://www.fool.com/investing/general/2016/01/18/internet-of-things-in-2016-6-stats-everyone-should.aspx.

14. "What Exactly Is the Internet of Things?" March 5, 2014, http://www.slideshare.net/harborresearch/harbor-research-and-postscapes-infographic

15. Leo Sun, "Internet of Things in 2016: 6 Stats Everyone Should Know," Motley Fool, Jan. 18, 2016, http://www.fool.com/investing/general/2016/01/18/internet-of-things-in-2016-6-stats-everyone-should.aspx.

16. "Industrial Internet Insights Report for 2015," GE and Accenture, 2014, http://www.ge.com/digital/sites/default/files/industrial-internet-insights-report.pdf.

17. Paul Roehrig and Ben Pring, "The Work Ahead: Mastering the Digital Economy," September 2016, https://www.cognizant.com/FoW/the-work-ahead.pdf.

18. "About GE Digital," GE, https://www.ge.com/digital/about-ge-digital.

19. Rick Clough, "GE Forms Digital Unit to Expand $6 Billion Software Business," *Bloomberg*, Sept. 14, 2015, http://www.bloomberg.com/news/articles/2015-09-14/ge-forms-digital-unit-to-expand-6-billion-software-business.

Chapter 3: There Will Be Blood

1. Carl Benedikt Frey and Michael A. Osborne, "The Future of Employment: How Susceptible Are Jobs to Computerisation?" University of Oxford, Sept. 17, 2013, http://www.oxfordmartin.ox.ac.uk/downloads/academic/The_Future_of_Employment.pdf.

2. Labor Force Statistics from the Current Population Survey, http://data.bls.gov/pdq/SurveyOutputServlet?request_action=wh&graph_name=LN_cpsbref1

3. The 2013 science fiction film *Elysium* (directed by Neill Blomkamp) depicts humanity divided between two classes of people: the ultra-rich living aboard a luxurious space station called Elysium, and the rest living a hardscrabble existence in Earth's ruins.

4. See Barack Obama, "The Way Ahead," *The Economist*, Oct, 8, 2016, http://www.economist.com/news/briefing/21708216-americas-president-writes-us-about-four-crucial-areas-unfinished-business-economic.

5. "The Future of Jobs, 2025: Working Side by Side with Robots: Automation Won't Destroy All the Jobs, But It Will Transform the Workforce—Including Yours," Aug. 24, 2015, https://www.forrester.com/The+Future+Of+Jobs+2025+Working+Side+By+Side+With+Robots/fulltext/-/E-RES119861

Chapter 4: The New Machine: Systems of Intelligence

1. "The Top 20 Valuable Facebook Statistics. Updated July 2016." Zephoria, https://zephoria.com/top-15-valuable-facebook-statistics/

2. We've based some of this discussion on Tim Urban, "The AI Revolution: The Road to Superintelligence," Wait But Why. Jan. 22, 2015, http://waitbutwhy.com/2015/01/artificial-intelligence-revolution-1.html.

3. Annalee Newitz, "What Is the Singularity, and Will You Live to See It?" io9, May 10, 2010, http://io9.gizmodo.com/5534848/what-is-the-singularity-and-will-you-live-to-see-it.

4. https://intelligence.org/2013/08/11/what-is-agi/

5. Chris Williams, "AI Guru Ng: Fearing a Rise of Killer Robots Is Like Worrying About Overpopulation on Mars," *The Register*, March 19, 2015, http://www.theregister.co.uk/2015/03/19/andrew_ng_baidu_ai/.

6. Wikipedia entries on ghost in the machine: https://en.wikipedia.org/wiki/Ghost_in_the_machine and https://en.wikipedia.org/wiki/The_Ghost_in_the_Machine.

7. "How Much Does the Internet Weigh?" YouTube, Oct. 29, 2011, https://www.youtube.com/watch?v=WaUzu-iksi8.

8. "2016 Global Internet Phenomena," Sandvine, June 2016, https://www.sandvine.com/trends/global-internet-phenomena/.

9. "Number of Netflix Streaming Subscribers Worldwide," Statista, 2016, http://www.statista.com/statistics/250934/quarterly-number-of-netflix-streaming-subscribers-worldwide/.

10. Xavier Amatriain, "How Does the Netflix Movie Recommendation Algorithm Work?" Quora, https://www.quora.com/How-does-the-Netflix-movie-recommendation-algorithm-work.

11. Yoni Heisler, "Netflix's Ratings System May Soon Be Getting a Big Overhaul," BGR, Jan. 11, 2016, http://bgr.com/2016/01/11/netflix-ratings-system-overhaul/.

12. Daniel Holloway, "Netflix Looks at Which Shows Are Most Binge-Watched," *Variety,* June 8, 2016, http://variety.com/2016/tv/news/netflix-looks-at-which-shows-are-most-binge-watched-1201791061/.

13. For a more complete description of the Netflix system, see "A 360 Degree View of The Entire Netflix Stack," High Scalability, Nov. 9, 2015, http://highscalability.com/blog/2015/11/9/a-360-degree-view-of-the-entire-netflix-stack.html.

14. Netflix socks: http://makeit.netflix.com/.

15. Daniel Weeks, "Netflix: Integrating Spark at Petabyte Scale," O'Reilly Conferences, Oct. 1, 2015, http://conferences.oreilly.com/strata/big-data-conference-ny-2015/public/schedule/detail/43373.

16. "How Much Is a Petabyte?" The Mozy Blog, July 2, 2009, https://mozy.com/blog/misc/how-much-is-a-petabyte/.

17. Tom Vanderbilt, "The Science Behind the Netflix Algorithms That Decide What You'll Watch Next," *Wired*, Aug. 7, 2013, http://www.wired.com/2013/08/qq_netflix-algorithm/

18. Alexis C. Madrigal, "How Netflix Reverse Engineered Hollywood," *The Atlantic*, Jan. 2, 2014, http://www.theatlantic.com/technology/archive/2014/01/how-netflix-reverse-engineered-hollywood/282679/ and Vincent Lanaria, "Netflix Has More Than 76,000 Micro-Genres of Movies and TV Shows: Here's How to Unlock Them," *Tech Times*, Jan. 9, 2016, http://www.techtimes.com/articles/122723/20160109/netflix-has-more-than-76000-micro-genres-of-movies-and-tv-shows-heres-how-to-unlock-them.htm.

19. "Netflix's Viewing Data: How We Know Where You Are in *House of Cards*," Netflix, Jan. 27, 2015, http://techblog.netflix.com/2015/01/netflixs-viewing-data-how-we-know-where.html and http://www.slideshare.net/PhilipFisherOgden/netflix-viewing-data-architecture-evolution-qcon-2014.

20. Yevgeniy Sverdlik, "Netflix Shuts Down Final Bits of Own Data Center Infrastructure," *Data Center Knowledge*, Feb. 11, 2016, http://www.datacenterknowledge.com/archives/2016/02/11/netflix-shuts-down-final-bits-of-own-data-center-infrastructure/.

21. Peter C. Evans and Rahul C. Basole, "Decoding the API Economy with Visual Analytics," The Center for Global Enterprise, Sept. 2, 2015, http://thecge.net/decoding-the-api-economy-with-visual-analytics/.

22. New business services integrate human process work (the smart hands) with collaboration and automation via technology platforms (the smart robots). See our white paper "Smart Hands and Smart Robots," https://www.cognizant.com/content/dam/Cognizant_Dotcom/worldwide_olt_pdf/Smart-Hands-and-Smart-Robots.pdf.

23. For example, DenialsIQ is built on Predix to focus on U.S. healthcare claims management. Hive (which runs on the perfectly named Honeycomb AI platform from British Gas) is a system that helps homeowners manage their IoT-enabled residence. See Chris Merriman, "Hive Launches First Products Built on Its Honeycomb IoT platform," *The Inquirer*, Jan. 27, 2016, http://www.theinquirer.net/inquirer/news/2443443/hive-launches-first-products-built-on-its-honeycomb-iot-platform.

24. Google's Cloud Machine Learning Products: https://cloud.google.com/products/machine-learning/.

25. Amazon Machine Learning: https://aws.amazon.com/machine-learning/.

Chapter 5: Your New Raw Materials: Data Is Better than Oil

1. http://www.datasciencecentral.com/profiles/blogs/that-s-data-science-airbus-puts-10-000-sensors-in-every-single

2. http://www.makeuseof.com/tag/memory-sizes-gigabytes-terabytes-petabytes/

3. Geoffrey Moore, "Is Your Business Model Being Disrupted? The Era of Code Halos Is Here," Cognizant Technology Solutions, Feb. 28, 2014, https://www.youtube.com/watch?v=hfKysCb3ju8

4. Jude Clemente, "How Much Oil Does the World Have Left?" Forbes, June 25, 2015, http://www.forbes.com/sites/judeclemente/2015/06/25/how-much-oil-does-the-world-have-left/#2af33c85dc5e.

5. See Thomas Davenport's bio, http://www.tomdavenport.com/about/ and Thomas Davenport, "The New World of Business Analytics," International Institute for Analytics, March 2010, http://www.sas.com/resources/asset/IIA_NewWorldofBusinessAnalytics_March2010.pdf.

6. See our white paper, "The Value of Signal (and the Cost of Noise): The New Economics of Meaning-Making," http://www.futureofwork.com/images/article/documents/the-value-of-signal.pdf.

7. Moore's law states that overall processing power for computers will double every two years.

8. Software "unicorns" are private venture-backed start-ups valued at $1 billion or more.

9. Joanna Rothkopf, "UberYACHT Is Real," Jezebel, April 28, 2016, http://jezebel.com/uberyacht-is-real-1773607160.

10. Paul Roehrig and Ben Pring, "The Work Ahead: Mastering the Digital Economy," September 2016, https://www.cognizant.com/FoW/the-work-ahead.pdf.

11. In the study, we surveyed leaders from 2,000 companies from across the globe with a combined total revenue of about $7.3 trillion during the past year. Approximately 6% of that revenue was driven by digital. While that percentage may sound small, it translates into roughly $438 billion. Over the next year, leaders believe they could unlock an additional $151.6 billion in revenue value if they took full advantage of digital. (Equivalent to an average impact of $75.7 million per studied company.) Executives expect the total potential revenue impact to more than double over the next three years to 11.4% of total revenue, unlocking value of about $770 billion per year. That's a total economic impact of about $2.3 trillion projected over the next three years across all companies studied. Extrapolating these findings across the industries

studied revealed that the impact of digital transformation over the next three years alone could be up to $20 trillion.

Chapter 6: Digital Business Models: Your Five Ways to Beat Silicon Valley

1. Henry Blodget, "Buffett on Newspapers," Business Insider, May 4, 2009, http://www.businessinsider.com/henry-blodget-buffett-on-newspapers-2009-5.
2. Marisa Garcia, "SAS CEO Says He Wants Real Digital Change at Airlines Not 'Lipstick on a Pig,'" Skift, April 21, 2016, https://skift.com/2016/04/21/sas-ceo-says-he-wants-real-digital-change-at-airlines-not-lipstick-on-a-pig/.
3. Stonewall Jackson Quotes, HistoryNet, http://www.historynet.com/stonewall-jackson-quotes
4. Robert Hoyle Brown, "Digital Process Acupuncture: How Small Changes Can Heal Business, and Spark Big Results," Cognizant Technology Solutions, February 2016, https://www.cognizant.com/whitepapers/Digital-Process-Acupuncture-How-Small-Changes-Can-Heal-Business-and-Spark-Big-Results-codex1438.pdf.
5. Malcolm Frank, Paul Roehrig and Ben Pring, *Code Halos: How the Digital Lives of People, Things, and Organizations Are Changing the Rules of Business* (Hoboken, NJ: John Wiley & Sons, 2014), https://www.amazon.com/Code-Halos-Organizations-Changing-Business/dp/1118862074/.
6. Madhumita Murgia, "Marc Andreessen: 'In 20 Years, Every Physical Item Will Have a Chip Implanted in It," *The Telegraph,* Dec. 23, 2015, http://www.telegraph.co.uk/technology/internet/12050185/Marc-Andreessen-In-20-years-every-physical-item-will-have-a-chip-implanted-in-it.html.
7. Tom Foster, "Kevin Plank Is Betting Almost $1 Billion That Under Armour Can Beat Nike," *Inc.,* http://www.inc.com/magazine/201602/tom-foster/kevin-plank-under-armour-spending-1-billion-to-beat-nike.html.
8. Frans van Houten, "How Technology Will Transform Healthcare," World Economic Forum, Jan. 19, 2016, https://www.weforum.org/agenda/2016/01/rethinking-healthcare-with-the-help-of-technology/.
9. "GE's Jeff Immelt on Digitizing in the Industrial Space," McKinsey & Co., October 2015, http://www.mckinsey.com/business-functions/organization/our-insights/ges-jeff-immelt-on-digitizing-in-the-industrial-space.

10. "Toyota Expands Focus on Software- and Data-Driven Mobility with Toyota Connected," Toyota press release, April 4, 2016, http://corporatenews.pressroom.toyota.com/releases/toyota+software+mobility+connected.htm.
11. Chris Ziegler and Nilay Patel, "Meet the New Ford, a Silicon Valley Software Company," The Verge, April 7, 2016, http://www.theverge.com/2016/4/7/11333288/ford-ceo-mark-fields-interview-electric-self-driving-car-software.

Chapter 7: Automate: The Robots Aren't Coming; They're Here

1. Robert Hoyle Brown, "Digital Process Acupuncture: How Small Changes Can Heal Business, and Spark Big Results," Cognizant Technology Solutions, February 2016, https://www.cognizant.com/whitepapers/Digital-Process-Acupuncture-How-Small-Changes-Can-Heal-Business-and-Spark-Big-Results-codex1438.pdf.
2. "Robotic Automation: Case Study," Robohub, http://robohub.org/wp-content/uploads/2015/01/Blue-Prism-Case-Study-for-Robohub.pdf.
3. In our study of 2,000 global companies, we calculated the laggard penalty by analyzing the difference in cost and revenue performance of digital "leaders" and "laggards." We found that individual laggard companies would miss out on about $692 million vs. their leader peers between 2015 and 2018.
4. According to Schumpeter, the "gale of creative destruction" describes the "process of industrial mutation that incessantly revolutionizes the economic structure from within, incessantly destroying the old one, incessantly creating a new one." (Source: Wikipedia entry on Joseph Schumpeter.)
5. Matt Egan, "Robots Write Thousands of News Stories a Year, but Not This One," CNN, June 11, 2015, http://money.cnn.com/2015/06/11/media/robots-journalists-media-jobs/.
6. Automated Insights website, https://automatedinsights.com/.
7. This news story, from the OakRidger local newspaper on May 7, 2013, carried a byline of "By Narrative Science and GameChanger Media," http://www.oakridger.com/article/20130507/SPORTS/130509938.
8. James Kotecki, "Take Me Out to the Ballgame," Automated Insights, July 17, 2016, https://automatedinsights.com/blog/take-automated-ball-game-next-chapter-ai-ap-partnership/

9. Chris Dixon, "What's Next in Computing?" Medium.com, Feb. 21, 2016, https://medium.com/software-is-eating-the-world/what-s-next-in-computing-e54b870b80cc#.we598fxrh.

10. "National Health Expenditures 2014 Highlights," Centers for Medicare & Medicaid Services, https://www.cms.gov/research-statistics-data-and-systems/statistics-trends-and-reports/nationalhealthexpenddata/downloads/highlights.pdf.

11. Donald Berwick and Andrew Hackbarth, "Eliminating Waste in U.S. Healthcare," *JAMA*, Vol. 307, No. 14, April 11, 2012, http://www.oregon.gov/oha/analytics/MetricsDocs/Eliminating_Waste_in_US_Health_Care.pdf.

12. We're not going into detail here about the new product-development process. There are plenty of other books and experts in the market.

13. For more in-depth ideas about building a practice for new products and services, a good place to look is Eric Ries, *The Lean Startup: How Today's Entrepreneurs Use Continuous Innovation to Create Radically Successful Businesses*, Crown Business, Sept. 13, 2011.

Chapter 8: Halo: Instrument Everything, Change the Game

1. James Sullivan, "Can Under Armour Meet CEO Kevin Plank's Ambitious Goal?" *The Motley Fool*, March 2, 2016, http://www.fool.com/investing/general/2016/03/02/can-under-armour-inc-meet-ceo-kevin-planks-goal.aspx.

2. Malcolm Frank, Paul Roehrig, and Ben Pring, *Code Halos: How the Digital Lives of People, Things, and Organizations Are Changing the Rules of Business* (Hoboken, NJ: John Wiley & Sons, 2014).

3. James Detar, "GE Sees Digital Revenue More Than Doubling to $15 Billion By 2020," *Investor's Business Daily*, June 23, 2016, http://www.investors.com/news/ge-courts-silicon-valley-investors-for-digital-industrial-push/.

4. Kristin Kloberdanz, "GE's Got a Ticket to Ride: How the Cloud Will Take Trains into a New Era," GE Reports, March 29, 2016, http://www.gereports.com/the-digital-railroad-how-the-cloud-will-take-trains-into-a-new-era/.

5. Lucinda Shen, "Immelt: 'There's Going to Be Trillions of Dollars of Wealth Created in the Industrial Internet," *Business Insider*, Dec. 3, 2015, http://www.businessinsider.com/ges-jeff-immelt-on-internet-strategy-2015-12.

6. Geoffrey Grider, "Over 10,000 People Have Now Received a Permanent Human RFID Microchip Implant," Sept. 4, 2015, http://www.nowtheendbegins.com/over-10000-people-have-now-received-a-permanent-human-rfid-microchip-implant/ and Lindsey Hoshaw, "Millions of Americans Use Medical Devices That May Be Vulnerable to Hacking," KQED Science, Aug. 3, 2015, https://ww2.kqed.org/futureofyou/2015/08/03/millions-of-americans-use-medical-devices-that-are-vulnerable-to-hacking/.

7. Thomas Davenport and D.J. Patil, "Data Scientist: The Sexiest Job of the 21st Century," *Harvard Business Review*, October 2012, https://hbr.org/2012/10/data-scientist-the-sexiest-job-of-the-21st-century/.

8. Euan Davis, "People—Not Just Machines—Will Power Digital Innovation," Cognizant Technology Solutions, April 2016, https://www.cognizant.com/whitepapers/People-Not-Just-Machines-Will-Power-Digital-Innovation-codex1850.pdf.

9. "Acqui-hiring" is the practice of acquiring a company primarily for the skills of its staff rather than for its product.

10. The trillion-dollar club includes six companies—Google, Amazon, Apple, Facebook, Netflix, Pandora—that have collectively made $1 trillion in market capitalization during the past 10 years, through leveraging the digital information provided by their customers.

11. Richard Hunter, *World Without Secrets*, (Hoboken, NJ: John Wiley & Sons, 2002), https://www.amazon.com/World-Without-Secrets-Ubiquitous-Computing/dp/0471218162.

12. Kim Zetter, "The Year's 11 Biggest Hacks, From Ashley Madison to OPM," *Wired*, December 23, 2015, https://www.wired.com/2015/12/the-years-11-biggest-hacks-from-ashley-madison-to-opm/

13. Steven Musil, "Sony Hack Leaked 47,000 Social Security Numbers, Celebrity Data," Cnet, Dec. 4, 2014, https://www.cnet.com/news/sony-hack-said-to-leak-47000-social-security-numbers-celebrity-data/.

14. Jonathan Martin and Alan Rappeport, "Debbie Wasserman Schultz to Resign DNC Post," *New York Times*, July 24, 2016, http://www.nytimes.com/2016/07/25/us/politics/debbie-wasserman-schultz-dnc-wikileaks-emails.html.

15. Jeff John Roberts, "Yahoo Has Been Hacked: What You Need to Know," *Fortune*, September 22, 2016, http://fortune.com/2016/09/22/yahoo-hack-qa/

16. Samuel Gibbs, "European Parliament Approves Tougher Data Privacy Laws," *Guardian*, April 14, 2016, https://www.theguardian.com/

technology/2016/apr/14/european-parliament-approve-tougher-data-privacy-rules.

17. Devlin Barrett, "FBI Plans to Keep Apple iPhone Hacking Method Secret," *The Wall Street Journal*, April 26, 2016, http://www.wsj .com/articles/fbi-plans-to-keep-apple-iphone-hacking-method-secret-sources-say-1461694735.

18. Statista portal, http://www.statista.com/statistics/264810/number-of-monthly-active-facebook-users-worldwide/.

19. Shannon Pettypiece, "Amazon Passes Walmart as Biggest Retailer by Market Value," Bloomberg, July 23, 2015, http://www.bloomberg .com/news/articles/2015-07-23/amazon-surpasses-wal-mart-as-biggest-retailer-by-market-value.

20. Lucy Hooker, "How Did Google Become the World's Most Valuable Company?" BBC, Feb. 11, 2016, http://www.bbc.com/news/business-35460398.

21. For more on our study, see Manish Bahl, "The Business Value of Trust," Cognizant Technology Solutions, May 2016, https://www.cognizant .com/whitepapers/The-Business-Value-of-Trust-codex1951.pdf.

22. "World's Biggest Data Breaches," Information Is Beautiful, Sept. 4, 2016, http://www.informationisbeautiful.net/visualizations/worlds-biggest-data-breaches-hacks/.

23. Shalini Ramachandran and Suzanne Vranica, "Comcast Seeks to Harness Trove of TV Data," *The Wall Street Journal*, Oct. 20, 2015, http://www.wsj .com/articles/comcast-seeks-to-harness-trove-of-tv-data-1445333401.

24. Michael Zakaras, "Why Our Health System Talks Up (but Actually Fears) Disruptive Innovation," *Forbes*, Oct. 23, 2015, http://www .forbes.com/sites/ashoka/2015/10/23/why-our-health-system-talks-up-but-actually-fears-disruptive-innovation/#6d7ceddd32a5.

Chapter 9: Enhance: Amplify Human Performance with the New Machine

1. Amy is an AI-based personal assistant from x.ai, a VC-funded technology company in New York City.

2. Erik Brynjolfsson and Andrew McAfee, *Race Against the Machine: How the Digital Revolution Is Accelerating Innovation, Driving Productivity, and Irreversibly Transforming Employment and the Economy* (Lexington, MA: Digital Frontier, 2012).

3. Cade Metz, "In Two Moves, AlphaGo and Lee Sedol Redefined the Future," *Wired*, March 16, 2016, http://www.wired.com/2016/03/ two-moves-alphago-lee-sedol-redefined-future/.

4. "Inspiring Zappos Customer Support Stories," SlideShare, Oct. 28, 2013, http://www.slideshare.net/InfinitOInc/10-inspiring-zappos-customer-support-stories.

5. Peter Moore, "Pret A Manager: Behind the Scenes at the 'Happy Factory,'" *Guardian,* April 14, 2015, https://www.theguardian.com/small-business-network/2015/apr/14/pret-a-manger-happy-coffee-chain.

6. David Aaker, "The Genius Bar—Branding the Innovation," *Harvard Business Review,* Jan. 5, 2012, https://hbr.org/2012/01/the-genius-bar-branding-the-in.

7. Stacy Liberatore, "Now Anyone Can Be an Iron Man," *Daily Mail,* Mar. 18, 2016, http://www.dailymail.co.uk/sciencetech/article-3499462/Now-Iron-Man-Panasonic-reveals-exoskeletons-allow-wearer-run-like-ninja-lift-heavy-objects.html.

8. Saurabh Jha, "Will Computers Replace Radiologists?" *Medscape,* May 12, 2016, http://www.medscape.com/viewarticle/863127.

9. Tom Simonite, "IBM's Automated Radiologist Can Read Images and Medical Records," *MIT Technology Review,* Feb. 4, 2016, https://www.technologyreview.com/s/600706/ibms-automated-radiologist-can-read-images-and-medical-records/.

Chapter 10: Abundance: Finding Your 10X Opportunities with the New Machine

1. Wikipedia entry on Narayana Health: https://en.wikipedia.org/wiki/Narayana_Health.

2. http://www.pbs.org/newshour/updates/india-doctor/

3. Ketaki Gokhale, "Heart Surgery in India for $1,583 Costs $106,385 in U.S.," *Bloomberg,* July 28, 2013, http://www.bloomberg.com/news/articles/2013-07-28/heart-surgery-in-india-for-1-583-costs-106-385-in-u-s-

4. N. Madhavan, "Compassionate Heart, Business Mind," *Business Today,* May 25, 2014, http://www.businesstoday.in/magazine/cover-story/biggest-india-innovation-narayana-health/story/205823.html.

5. Geeta Anand, "The Henry Ford of Heart Surgery," *The Wall Street Journal,* Nov. 25, 2009, http://www.wsj.com/articles/SB125875892887958111.

6. One of our nominations for the "Best Book You (Probably) Haven't Read" is Juan Enriquez and Steve Gullans' *Evolving Ourselves: How Unnatural Selection and Nonrandom Mutation Are Changing Life on Earth* (New York: Penguin Publishing, 2015).

7. Sarah Mahoney, "Walgreens' Telehealth Grows As We Warm to Digital Doctors," *MediaPost,* Nov. 12, 2015, http://www.mediapost .com/publications/article/262453/walgreens-telehealth-grows-as-we-warm-to-digital.html.

8. "Enduring Ideas: The Three Horizons of Growth," *McKinsey Quarterly,* December 2009, http://www.mckinsey.com/business-functions/strategy-and-corporate-finance/our-insights/enduring-ideas-the-three-horizons-of-growth.

9. Eugene Kim, "The Epic 30-Year Bromance of Billionaire CEOs Larry Ellison and Marc Benioff," *Business Insider,* Aug. 12, 2015, http://www .businessinsider.com/larry-ellison-marc-benioff-relationship-2015-8/ #when-benioff-first-started-building-salesforce-in-1999-he-was-still-working-at-oracle-he-says-ellison-was-always-supportive-of-his-outside-endeavor-giving-him-permission-to-split-work-at-salesforce-in-the-morning-and-at-oracle-in-the-afternoons-ellison-even-let-benioff-take-a-6-month-sabbatical-before-starting-salesforce-6.

10. Salesforce.com positioned itself in the market as the antidote to Oracle and other ERP vendors. See also Patrick Hoge, "The Benioff-Ellison Divide: It's About More than Salesforce vs. Oracle," *Upstart Business Journal* from *San Francisco Business Times,* April 18, 2014, http://upstart .bizjournals.com/entrepreneurs/hot-shots/2014/04/18/meet-marc-benioff-the-anti-ellison.html?page=all.

11. LVMH is itself majority owned by Christian Dior.

12. Tim Bajarin, "Why the Maker Movement Is Important to America's Future," *Time,* May 19, 2014, http://time.com/104210/maker-faire-maker-movement/.

13. Josh Ong, "Apple Co-Founder Offered First Computer Design to HP 5 Times," *Apple Insider,* Dec. 6, 2010, http://appleinsider.com/articles/10/12/ 06/apple_co_founder_offered_first_computer_design_to_hp_5_times.

14. Tom Foster, "Kevin Plank Is Betting Almost $1 Billion That Under Armour Can Beat Nike," *Inc.,* February 2016, http://www.inc.com/ magazine/201602/tom-foster/kevin-plank-under-armour-spending-1-billion-to-beat-nike.html.

15. Wikipedia entry on Frederick Winslow Taylor: https://en.wikipedia .org/wiki/Frederick_Winslow_Taylor.

Chapter 11: Discovery: Manage Innovation for the Digital Economy

1. "The Sports Market," May 2011, https://www.atkearney.com/fr/ communications-media-technology/ideas-insights/article/-/asset_ publisher/LCcgOeS4t85g/content/the-sports-market/10192.

2. Wikipedia entry on Thomas Lord: https://en.wikipedia.org/wiki/Thomas_Lord.

3. Stephen Adams, "Jane Austen Wrote About Baseball 40 Years Before It Was 'Invented'," *Telegraph*, November 2008, http://www.telegraph.co.uk/culture/books/3562873/Jane-Austen-wrote-about-baseball-40-years-before-it-was-invented.html.

4. Kurt Badenhausen, "Cristiano Ronaldo Is First Athlete with 200 Million Social Media Followers," *Forbes*, Feb 23, 2016, http://www.forbes.com/sites/kurtbadenhausen/2016/02/23/cristiano-ronaldo-is-the-first-athlete-with-200-million-social-media-followers/#57b26a661129.

5. From Mark Zuckerberg's Facebook page, March 25, 2014, https://m.facebook.com/zuck/posts/10101319050523971.

6. Madhumita Murgia, "Inside Netflix: How Reed Hastings Is Building the First Global TV Network," *Telegraph*, March 26, 2016, http://www.telegraph.co.uk/technology/2016/03/26/inside-netflix-how-reed-hastings-is-building-the-first-global-tv/.

7. "The Law of Accelerating Returns," Kurzweil Accelerating Intelligence, March 7, 2001, http://www.kurzweilai.net/the-law-of-accelerating-returns.

8. Porta Crow, "Wall Street Is Obsessed with This Technology That No One Quite Understands—Here's the Best Explanation We've Seen," *Business Insider*, March 13, 2016, http://www.businessinsider.com/what-is-blockchain-barclays-2016-3.

9. Joe Blevins, "Carl Sagan Did Say 'Billions and Billions' a Lot on Cosmos, Video Proves," *A.V. Club*, Jan. 12, 2015, http://www.avclub.com/article/carl-sagan-did-say-billions-and-billions-lot-cosmo-213673.

10. "Laurence D. Fink's 2016 Corporate Governance Letter," http://www.nytimes.com/interactive/2016/02/02/business/dealbook/document-larry-finks-2016-corporate-governance-letter.html?_r=0.

11. Robert Hoyle Brown, "Digital Process Acupuncture: How Small Changes Can Heal Business, and Spark Big Results," Cognizant Technology Solutions, February 2016, https://www.cognizant.com/whitepapers/Digital-Process-Acupuncture-How-Small-Changes-Can-Heal-Business-and-Spark-Big-Results-codex1438.pdf.

12. Question on Quora: https://www.quora.com/How-often-do-Hollywood-movies-lose-money#.

13. Deborah Gage, "The Venture Capital Secret: 3 Out of 4 Start-Ups Fail," *The Wall Street Journal*, Sept. 20, 2012, http://www.wsj.com/news/articles/SB10000872396390443720204578004980476429190.

14. "In Praise of Failure," Benedict Evans blog, Aug. 10, 2016, http://ben-evans.com/benedictevans/2016/4/28/winning-and-losing?

15. Carroll Lachnit, "Five Myths About Stick Shifts: Manual vs Automatic Transmissions," Edmunds.com, Sept. 26, 2013, http://www.edmunds.com/fuel-economy/five-myths-about-stick-shifts.html.

16. Google announcement, Google Plus, March 28, 2012, https://plus.google.com/+google/posts/MVZBmrnzDio.

17. Yoko Kubota, "Toyota Again No. 1 in Global Car Sales," *MarketWatch*, Jan. 26, 2016, http://www.marketwatch.com/story/toyota-again-no-1-in-global-car-sales-2016-01-26.

18. Yoko Kubota, "Behind Toyota's Late Shift Into Self-Driving Cars," *The Wall Street Journal*, Jan. 12, 2016, http://www.wsj.com/articles/behind-toyotas-late-shift-into-self-driving-cars-1452649436.

19. Sebastian Toma, "Toyota Announces Billion-Dollar Investment In Self-Driving Car Technology," *Autoevolution*, June 20, 2016, http://www.autoevolution.com/news/toyota-announces-billion-dollar-investment-in-self-driving-car-technology-108699.html.

20. Marie Kondo, *The Life-Changing Magic of Tidying Up* (New York: Ten Speed Press, 2014). https://www.amazon.com/Life-Changing-Magic-Tidying-Decluttering-Organizing/dp/1607747308.

Chapter 12: Competing on Code: A Call to Action from the Future

1. Ray Kurzweil, "The Law of Accelerating Returns," Kurzweil Accelerating Intelligence, March 7, 2001, http://www.kurzweilai.net/the-law-of-accelerating-returns.

2. Monica Nickelsburg, "A12 CEO Oren Etzioni Envisions an Artificial Intelligence 'Utopia,'" GeekWire, March 30, 2016, http://www.geekwire.com/2016/ai2-ceo-oren-etzioni-envisions-artificial-intelligence-utopia/.

3. Michael Sainato, "Stephen Hawking, Elon Musk and Bill Gates Warn about Artificial Intelligence," *Observer*, Aug. 19, 2015, http://observer.com/2015/08/stephen-hawking-elon-musk-and-bill-gates-warn-about-artificial-intelligence/.

4. Wikipedia page on intelligence: https://en.wikipedia.org/wiki/Intelligence.

5. James Bates, "Guide to League of Legends," *ESPN*, Jan. 14, 2016, http://es.pn/1Pfg9rE.

6. Alex Davies, "Maven, GM's Car-Sharing Scheme, Is Really about a Driverless Future," *Wired*, Jan. 21, 2016, http://bit.ly/1QfNSEs.

7. Alexander Sword, "Speed Is the New Currency of Business," *Computer Business Review*, Jan. 20, 2016, http://bit.ly/1nBOLy1.

8. Matthew Leising, "Blythe Masters Firm Raises Cash, Wins Australian Contract," *Bloomberg*, Jan. 21, 2016, http://bloom.bg/1OJrYH2.

9. Harrison Kaminsky, "Listen to This AI-composed Song in the Style of The Beatles," *Digital Trends*, September 24, 2016, http://www .digitaltrends.com/music/sony-composes-music-artificial-intelligence-style-the-beatles/.

10. Andrew Follett, "Scientists Use Quantum Mechanics to Teleport Particle 4 Miles," *Daily Caller* New Foundation, Sep. 26, 2016, http://dailycaller.com/2016/09/26/canadians-use-quantum-mechanics-to-teleport-particle-4-miles/#ixzz4MzdmNJbs.

11. Wikipedia page on Maslow's hierarchy of needs: https://en.wikipedia .org/wiki/Maslow%27s_hierarchy_of_needs.

Index

Note: Page references in *italics* refer to figures.